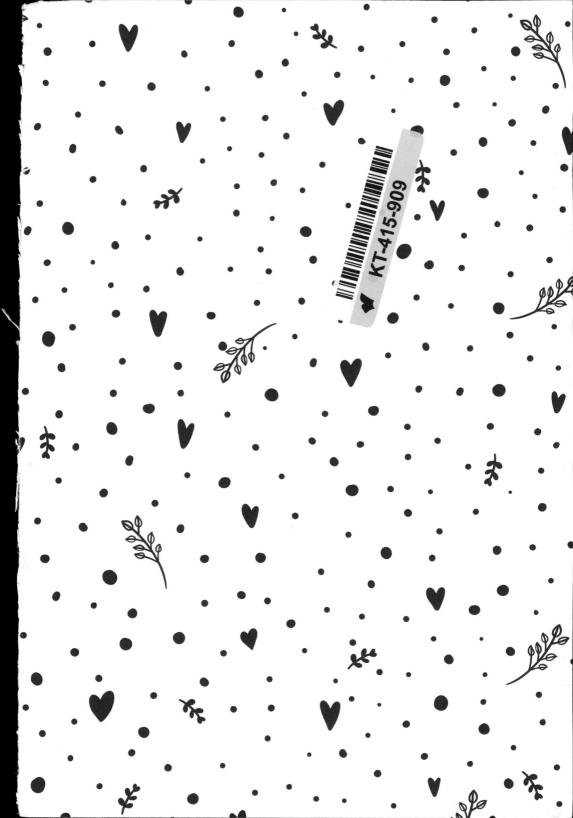

Tap to Tidy

♡

STACEY SOLOMON

Tap to Tidy

ORGANISING, CRAFTING
& CREATING HAPPINESS
IN A MESSY WORLD

EBURY
PRESS

Obviously everything in my life is dedicated to my Pickles. But this book isn't just for them, as much as I love them, this one is for you, too. For each and every one of you who gave me the courage to put it all into writing and share my weirdness with the world. I am forever grateful. Loads of Love.

Stace

♡

Contents

A Quick Hello

My Tap to Tidy Day

Good Morning!

Time For Me

Tidy Outdoors

Easy Afternoons

Happy Hometime

Time Together

Making Every Day Special

Seasonal Tap to Tidys

A Quick Hello ♡

Storage jars. Glue guns. Labels. And don't even get me started on my trusty tension rods! Welcome to my world... that I just love to tidy and organise.

If you've picked up this book, you probably already know that about me. I'm the one you'll find busy clipping my crisp packets to curtain hooks in the snack cupboard (in colour order, of course) or spending Saturday night with my Hoover (and a Diet Coke in a champagne glass, too. Wild, I know!). What you may not know, though, is *why* I bloomin' love it – and why I'm hoping that, through these pages, you can enjoy it with me, too!

I really do get so much joy from crafting, tidying and organising the crap out of life. I love nothing better than to see a messy corner transform into a happy, tidy space, to know that the junk drawer is finally sorted, or to turn my old candle jars into beautiful vases. It doesn't have to be something monumental either, just making the bed in the morning, or sometimes the afternoon, makes me feel like the day is going OK. Some nights, Joe and I are joined by all of the boys, so we'll wake in the morning and the bed is a complete tip. It's the most satisfying thing to just tuck the sheets in, put the throw over and chuck the pillows on (well, I say chuck, they're actually all *placed*). I can't tell you how much I love that. It may not seem a lot, but to me, with a baby and two older boys, a job, a cat, a dog and a Joe, it feels like a massive achievement.

As a working mum, being tidy and organised definitely helps life run that much smoother. If things are tidy and organised and in a working system, my brain feels clearer, I feel as though I'm more on top of things and I know exactly what I need to do to stay in control. Well, most of the time.

But it's much more than that, crafting, tidying and organising is something I do for *me*. Honestly, it's not just the end result that makes me happy, it's the process that I get something from. It's a bit of time for me. Time to take my mind off whatever I might

2

be worried about. It lets me focus on what's right in front of me. Tidying is the process, and being organised is the result, and the most important thing of all is that I feel good about things – calmer, happier and more in control. That's what I'm so excited to share with you here. But above all, I hope that this book gives you a moment for you, because G-d knows, you deserve it.

♡ Tidy By Nature ♡

I've always been quite scatty, so being organised is a necessity for my personality. I need to know where everything is and I wouldn't say that this has ever ruled my life, but it's always been a big part of it.

When I was little, I used to sort through all my toys and make sure they were in the right boxes, and at mealtimes I would separate my food into little sections on my plate. My mum says she thought, what the hell? (I still do it now: if I'm having a roast dinner, all the different foods have to be arranged into separate sections so I can get exactly what I want on my fork – a piece of potato, a piece of meat and a piece of veg, each time, thank you.) Later, as a teenager, I stayed tidy and organised – lazy, but organised! My college still uses some of my old exercise books as examples for their current students, because they're all really neat and set out exactly as they're supposed to be. Although I have to admit that this was during my college years, after I'd had Zach, and being tidy and organised became more urgent than ever. Put it this way, none of my secondary school teachers would show me as an example for the model student! Proof that we're all growing...

I definitely get that side of me from my mum. My mum is really organised, even more so than me – and taught me to be the same way. It was all part of learning to be responsible for myself. Growing up, if I forgot to pack a piece of homework or a part of my PE kit for school, it would be *my* responsibility. I quickly learnt that if I didn't get myself together, I'd never have the right stuff for lessons and would end up in detention every day.

GETTING MY SH♥T TOGETHER

And then at a really young age – I was just 17 when I became pregnant – I became a mum myself. That meant there was me, my brother, my sister, my baby son, Zachary, and my mum all living in one small house. Now there was no bloomin' room to be messy! But more than that, I felt completely out of control and out of my depth. I just had no idea what the hell I was doing. I felt as if all my decisions had been made for me and there was nothing I could do about that.

There were only tiny things that I could control, which might be, say, to make up the bottles, or to sort through the nappies and wet wipes. So, I ended up becoming even more into taking care of the little things – that, handily, kept my mind busy, because I really didn't know where I was or who I was for a long moment.

It was also a time in my life when I didn't really have anything – as a teenage mum, I was on working tax credits. So, I would collect my Giro (as the cheques were called) and have to be really organised with my money to make sure that I could afford everything that I needed. For instance, I'd get milk vouchers from the government to buy formula for the baby, but I only got a certain amount. I had to be really strict about what type of milk I was going to buy and where I was going to get it from (it definitely doesn't all cost the same) and how I was going to use it.

And that was just one of the ways I really *had* to get it together: to become more vigilant about what I was doing, what I was spending, what I had in already, so that when I went to the shops I didn't buy anything I didn't need. I found it all difficult, because I was really sad and struggling: asking myself, what have I done? The only thing that kept me going was knowing I had no choice but to get myself together for this little human that I loved so much. Even though, if I'm honest, I had no idea how to love him at the time.

LIFE WITH HOE AND THE PICKLES

That's stayed with me. These days, I'm in a much happier place and life is busy in a different way, with a career, my boys Zachary, Leighton and Rex, and my partner Joe (Hoe!). But I still like to have my snacks organised, my fridge organised, and I really like to plan our meals. If I'm not organised about it, I'll go out shopping and think, OK, we probably need bread or milk, and then I'll find out later there is a whole loaf of bread at home, or two full cartons of milk. So, I do think that aspect of my organising, the one that helps me avoid wasting food or money or time, comes from becoming a mum as a teenager and having the bare minimum to survive on, meaning I had to just make it stretch. While I'm lucky enough that I don't have those same worries today, I will never take it for granted, because who knows where life will take you?

Still, I don't do it just because I was brought up that way, or because I had to get my sh♥t together as a young mum. Even if my life wasn't so busy, tidying would be something I'd do anyway – and if a by-product of that is that I know what's going on and things can run a bit more smoothly, then great!

Nowadays, crafting, tidying and organising is genuinely something that I enjoy doing for *me* – it's my hobby, I suppose you could say, and my 'me time'. I can't tell you how excited I get about making something new from old bits and pieces I've cleared away. I just love that – I call them my 'make ups', and I will be showing you all sorts of things you can make up, too. So, hold onto those old Hoover parts you don't need any more.

♡ Yes, I Have Messy Days ♡ (And A Junk Trunk)

Now, before I go any further, a big disclaimer! My house is never completely tidy, ever. That's why I have to tidy! I don't organise things because I think they'll stay like that – they won't. And certain places are almost always messy: my cutlery drawer, the snack cupboard (because the kids go in it all day, every day…). That's OK – for me, some of the fun of it is reorganising it all. When the systems are in place, it's easy to put things back where they belong.

Also, for the record: I am Stacey Solomon and I am a hoarder. I'm not ashamed to say it. I've got a junk trunk outside my house, which Joe just thinks is the worst thing in the world. He calls it my toot trunk – 'Oh, it's full of toot.' Have you ever been to a toot shop? It's a shop that doesn't have a name, but it's like an Aladdin's cave of stuff. I love that kind of shop! And that is exactly what my junk trunk is. My very own toot shop in the garden.

Basically, you're supposed to put your bins in this trunk – you know, it's one of those big plastic boxes. But I don't have any bins in there. I just have stuff that *should* be in the bin but instead I've kept it! So, every time Joe uses a tin of beans, I'll think, 'Ooh, I'll have that' – and I wash it out and put it out in my junk trunk. As well as candles, finished toilet rolls, empty bottles of fabric softener, conditioner – anything I can get my hands on. The other day I found a broken hanger. I put it in the junk trunk, searched online for 'What can I make out of a broken hanger?' and later made a bedside lamp that I bloomin' love.

I love my junk trunk. Honestly, I get so excited to go in there. But I *have* to have an idea. And sometimes I'll get upset when I look in there and I think I've got nothing – nothing! I don't know what to do with you. So, I do upset myself. But then some days I open it up and I think, 'Ah! I know what I can do with that.'

I make something nearly every day. So, I am tidy, but I do hoard. There's definitely a formula to hoarding, so I'm going to share with you the things I think are worth stashing away. To hoard or not to hoard!

In a similar way, some days, I'm just so on it: I get up and think, I'm going to blitz this house. And some days I wake up and think, I cannot be bothered. I don't have the energy to tidy and I don't want to do it. I can see a messy corner or a pile of stuff and tell myself, I'm not even going to touch that, I don't have it in me. I just shut the door on it! Which doesn't mean I won't *ever* enjoy tidying again. It just means today is not the day. And that's OK. Nobody is going to wake up every day feeling the same motivation and having all the energy in the world.

♡ Tidying My Worries Away (No. Really) ♡

Some days I can feel just a little bit out of place, angsty, and not sure what I'm supposed to be doing… I call it 'trying to catch a breath': moments where I feel like I really can't take a full breath of air. And that's when I really like to sit down and focus on a task, because I find that it takes my mind away from anything that I'm worrying about – even if it's subconscious, because most of the time I'm worrying I don't even know what the hell I'm worrying about! The best thing for me is to take my mind away completely.

That's when I open a really messy cupboard or drawer or grab a glue gun and some junk, and I think, right, I know what I've got to do now. Suddenly, all I can focus on is: where should that thing go? What could I use this for? What should I organise these bits into? There are so many things I have to think about when I'm tidying that my mind focuses on the task in front of me, rather than anything else that might be whizzing around in my head.

So that's where my motivation stems from, when I feel a little on edge or breathless and need to focus on something else and do something that I enjoy. Ultimately, I do it not so everything around me looks lovely and tidy, but so that I feel better on the inside, too – for my mental health, you could say.

MY WAY OF MEDITATING

That's why I think tidying and organising is my form of meditation. Honestly, this is not a joke, but if I go to a spa, or someone says you've got to try this calming meditation – blah, blah, blah – I just can't lie there and think of nothing. I find it absolutely impossible. I end up thinking, 'Oh, I've got this thing to do later, will I get it done… and also, what if *that* other thing happens?' My brain will just not shut up! Things slip into my mind and out again, and it just doesn't work for me – I don't find it relaxing! But while I think traditional meditation might not be for everyone, I genuinely think there's some form of meditation for everyone. And mine is to completely focus on something – and that's what crafting, tidying and organising lets me do. When I'm sitting there, pulling everything out of a cupboard, looking at all the colours and the sizes of all the items I've got, working out how best they're going to go back in there, I'm not thinking of anything else other than the task at hand. My brain can't chatter away because it's too busy thinking about how it's going to achieve what is in front of me.

Recently, I've been trying to reteach myself the piano, after learning when I was younger. And that kind of focus works like meditation for me, too, because I can't possibly think of anything else other than trying to work out how to play the notes and make my hands go in the right places.

ENJOYING THE AFTERGLOW

When the tidying's done, there's the satisfaction of looking at somewhere that was once a tip and knowing I've just sorted that all out! There's a real sense of achievement. The gratification is just so good. I love that feeling: it makes me feel like I've accomplished something and, on top of that, like I'm in control. A lot of my anxiety probably comes from feeling very out of control – which might be the case for you, too. I think for a lot of us those worried feelings are about not being able to change certain things or make certain things happen. But, you *can* make little things happen in your own world. You really *are* in control of some things and you can achieve something that might seem small to somebody else, but feels really big to you. And I love that.

♡ Tap to Tidy ♡

When I started doing Tap to Tidy on Instagram, I had no idea people would enjoy it as much as me. Social media is meant to be a representation of what is going on in your day and I often feel like in between school runs and mealtimes all I would ever do is tidy. So I had nothing else to share! Thank G-d so many of us enjoy the satisfaction of seeing a huge mess turn into something liveable, because, quite frankly, it's the only content I've got most of the time.

Tap to Tidy for me started because, as a parent, sometimes you spend your days doing these tasks and they are thankless. No one says 'Well done!' or 'Wow, I can really see the difference!' because no one notices. And if you're lucky, the only reward is that it will stay tidy for more than an hour. So Tap to Tidys were my medal, my 'well done' to myself, the praise that I needed and the proof of how much I'd done to show Joe when he gets home.

It may seem petty, but I like having proof that I've done something, especially on days when I haven't been officially 'at work' but instead in the house with the Pickles (as I call the boys). It's also really nice to log how much housework I'm doing and I'd be lying if I said I haven't used it as ammunition in my arguments with Joe. You know, if he's ever wondered, 'What have you done today?' And I've been able to reply with a full document of evidence.

At first, I was posting stories about organising stuff that I had in the house. Early on, when I didn't have many followers, I remember sorting through my shells – yes, I've got a shell collection – and organising them into jars. But it was when I was pregnant with Rex, my youngest, and I sorted out my pantry that I think people really started noticing it as something I do. At the time, some thought I was nesting pre-baby, but of course, I would have been tidying that cupboard even if I wasn't pregnant.

I can't tell you the feeling when, after a while of sharing my Tap to Tidys, I was inundated with other people's. They began tagging me in their own 'Tap to Tidys', and it was like cupboard porn for me. Also, it was such a lovely sense of community, feeling like you belong somewhere and that there are people out there as enthusiastic about the things you love as you.

A Club Where Everyone's Welcome

I genuinely love seeing other people's Tap to Tidys; it makes me feel like there's a whole group of people who enjoy doing something that I enjoy – like we're in a club. I'm part of this little organising society where everyone shares their ideas and what they've achieved. We ask each other questions, too – sometimes I'll ask, what's the best way to do this? Or, does anyone know how to use these or what to do with those?

And vice versa. Just the other day, someone sent me a picture of this tiny space in her house, asking, how can I store my shoes in here? I sent her a video of my shoes, all hanging on a tension rod (you'll be hearing more about those) and explained that she could just shove one in that space. So we're sharing tips with each other, which I love.

Most of all, we're inspiring each other. These days, I get loads of messages from people saying, it really motivates me to see the Tap to Tidys, or, thank you for making me feel like I can do it and achieve it. And the truth is, I get the same from other people's, it really motivates me.

♡ How To Use This Book ♡

I would love you to be able to sit here, read this book and not feel any pressure to have to do anything at all, but just enjoy the satisfaction of reading about crafting, tidying and organising. I hope this story will let you switch off for a moment and just relax. Dip in, dip out, flick through to your favourite bits, whatever you want.

And if you do want to try out some tips or some of the things that I like to do, then it's here for that, too. Because I've got loads to tell you.

Right, now time to stop waffling. Let's make a cup of tea, grab a Daim Bar and do this.

'You can't go back and change the beginning but you can start where you are and change the ending.'

James R. Sherman

My Tap to Tidy Day ♡

Hello, I feel the first thing I need to make clear is that Tap to Tidy is not just a way of organising my home, it applies to my whole life.

So many of us are juggling children, friends, family, jobs, relationships and everything else in between. I don't think I know anyone who hasn't got piles on their plate these days.

So I'm so excited to share with you my method to organising absolutely everything. From that space under the stairs you've been chucking things in for years, to that drawer full of wires that you think you probably shouldn't throw away (one of them's got to be important, hasn't it?). So here we go…

♡ The Tap to Tidy ♡ Method

Honestly, I know mess can be daunting. But it doesn't need to be! We're going to take this together, step by step – and starting with the simplest step of all.

1. FACE UP TO THE CHAOS

Faced with a pile of mess, the first thing to do is acknowledge that it's a pile of mess. That means you start thinking, right, this needs changing, I need to do this, let's just go for it! You're getting ready to...

2. GET IT ALL OUT!

When I finally get the time to actually tackle the mess, I take everything out, spreading it all across the floor to see what I've got. From my experience, just doing one cupboard or one section of a room at a time makes the task easier to achieve. If I ever try to tackle an entire room and all of its contents, I almost always get overwhelmed and want to give up. Deal with one cupboard, or drawer, or corner of a room at a time and take out *everything*. Even if you think, oh, that doesn't look too bad... get it out! Just get every single thing that you can out of that space and spread it across the floor.

3. Do A Mental Scan

Next, just look at it all for a little while. Take it in and start to ask yourself questions about what you've got. OK, what do I really want? What am I not that sure about? And keep asking. Where does this go? Does it belong here? Does it belong in another drawer/cupboard/room? Does it belong in the recycling? Does it belong to somebody else – will somebody else make more use of this? Or does it definitely belong in the bin because it's useless or unfixable or the sell-by date was 10 years ago?!

4. Sort It Out

Then, once you've thought about what you've got, put it all into piles. I'll usually do:

- Bin It
- Recycle
- Definitely Keeping
- Maybes (the stuff I still can't work out if I want to keep or not)

19

I might also have a Give It Away pile, if I'm tackling something like my wardrobe, where I'll offer stuff to friends or family or make a bag for charity.

5. CLEAN THE EMPTY SPACE

Since you've got everything out, you can actually clean the cupboard, drawer or space that you've tackled, ready for all your Definitely Keeping items.

6. FIND YOUR STUFF A HOME

Now you know what *should* be there, find a good home for your Definitely Keeping pile. That doesn't mean just sticking it all back in any old way. It will depend on what you're tidying, but I always like things to be as *visible* as possible (so I can still see what I've got) and *accessible* (so I can actually get to the stuff I use). As we go through my day, I'll show you exactly how I do this.

7. DEAL WITH THE MAYBES

Take a look at how much space you have left in front of you – because that's now going to help you deal with that Maybe pile. I'll only put back in what now feels *essential*, whether that's because I can't bear to throw it away or I think I'll still use it (and it fits in without messing up my nice organised cupboard or drawer). The rest of that Maybe stack can then go into the other piles of stuff I'm getting rid of: Bin, Recycle or Give It Away. Bag them up, and you're done!

And that's it! Don't worry if that sounds a lot – I'm going to talk you through how you'd put that technique to use in all sorts of different scenarios. Really, it's just what I've always done: I've always liked spreading things out and sorting through them! When we were little, my sister and brother would rummage through a box to find the doll that they wanted, but I always thought I was missing out on some special doll that could be in there if I just looked hard enough. So I'd empty the entire box on the floor to see every single doll before I finally chose the one I wanted to play with. I've always thought there's treasure everywhere – and sometimes it's even in your own home.

Today, sometimes I'll empty a cupboard and find things and think, I forgot I had that! And it's such an exciting feeling – well, I think so anyway. I've found so many treasures: perfumes I've forgotten I had (probably out of date but I'll still wear them) and handwritten notes. A couple of years ago, Joe wrote a letter to me for *Loose Women* – a jokey, silly love letter we read on air – and I took it home. The other day I found it and I thought, oh my G-d! That really got me excited.

So, here's how you can put it all into action…

♡ How To Tap to Tidy Anything ♡

Like I said, I do like to tackle one cupboard, drawer or corner at a time. But if you have a whole room that you look at and it just overwhelms you, don't worry. We've all got one! Mine's the shed in the garden that we've split into two: one side is a snug for the kids, while the other, smaller side is piled up to the brim with decorations – Christmas, Easter – because we don't have a loft or anything like that. And when I tackle the shed, I will give myself a few days to do it. Because it's outside, I probably can take everything out and lay it across the garden. But if it was a room inside the house or the space under the stairs, for example – which is often a place where people end up getting overwhelmed, because you just shove everything in there – the best thing to do is to break it down into smaller spaces. Say, right, I'm going to start on this corner. And don't even *think* about the whole room.

If you can't even get into the room? Then start at the doorway – that's absolutely fine. Just take out what's obstructing you from getting in there. Have a look at it. Ask yourself your questions – you're already at step three of the Tap to Tidy Method! Then, follow the rest of the steps to do what you've got to do with that stuff.

♥ ♥
♥ *Tip* don't stress over your Maybe pile. I promise you, once you've tidied and organised your space, your Maybe pile will become much clearer. You'll know what you're missing, what you have too much of and what you really want in that space, so the decisions become obvious.

Honestly, Tap to Tidy applies to absolutely anything, if you just follow the steps (you might even find you can skip a few). I've even used it to organise my apps on my phone. So, you get them all out – take all your apps out of any folders they are already in. You do your mental scan, thinking about what you've got. Sort through them, deleting any that you're not keeping. And then you find the survivors a home!

I organise mine by colour – going from blue to green, to yellow, orange, pink, red, white and black. So, the Facebook app is blue – it will be on my blue page; Instagram, that's pink, so it's on my pink page. There are a couple of miscellaneous apps on the last page that don't fit into any one colour category (which really upsets me; I almost deleted those apps!). The result is that your phone looks like a rainbow – but also you know exactly where *everything* is.

THE QUESTION OF CLUTTER: HOW TO KNOW WHAT TO KEEP AND WHAT TO CHUCK

Being organised doesn't mean living in a completely bare house with nothing in it. That said, you definitely go through cycles and phases of what you want and don't want around. Sometimes, I'll look at a shelf and there's too much on there. I've taken it too far! So I'll put some stuff away. But then after a while, I'll think, Oh, that's a bit bare and sad, and I'll bring stuff out again! It just depends on what mood I'm in.

♥ ♥

♥ *Tip* Don't think you've got to keep all your ornaments out – have a drawer for them, so you can take them out and put them back whenever you please.

That's why I find it difficult to throw things away: 1) Because you can always upcycle things that you love and make them something special, and 2) Your taste changes all the time and your mood can sometimes define what you want around you. For me, it can even be hormonal! I could be due on and not want anything out: I think, urgh, it's all messy. Equally, I could be in the best mood of my life and decide we need extra candles, and more fejkas everywhere! So it's good to have options. You don't have to choose to be one person or the other.

Little things I love: **Fejkas!**

You probably know how much I love my fejkas. It's what IKEA
(I'm always there) calls its fake potted plants. (I'm pretty sure
it means 'fake' in Swedish and I'm even more sure I don't
pronounce it right.) My house is *full* of them. I even have a
cupboard dedicated to fejkas.

That's talking about proper ornaments though – I don't ever
want my surfaces covered with a load of crap! Honest to G-d,
I've even started dressing my dining-room table, so no one can
put anything on it. For ages it was the bloomin' dump space.
People would come in from school, dump their bag on the
table; come in from work, dump their paperwork on the table. I
thought, what the hell is this?!

Then Joe came home from holiday – he'd been away for a week
with Harry, his little boy – and so I thought, I'm gonna make
us a nice dinner and lay the table. And I loved the look of it
so much, I left it all on there. And, I kid you not, it's stopped
everyone from dumping their stuff there. Now they can't leave
anything on the table because it's covered in placemats, candles,
glasses and fejkas. So they have to put it away.

♥ ♥

♥ *Tip* If there's a 'dumping space', fill it with something you want to look at and that makes you happy. Then no one can chuck their belongings there and ruin it!

WHY I LOVE TO REUSE, RECYCLE AND, YES, REGIFT!

If I *do* decide to get rid of something, I feel so much better about it if it lives on somewhere else. You can take a lot of household items to your local charity shop, or you can upcycle something into something else and give it to a friend as a gift (save your perfume bottles for my idea on page 56). Or just give it to them as it is! I know some people might think, well, *I* wouldn't want that. But I actually would – there are things in my friends' houses that if they brought them round, I'd be over the moon! One friend has a really nice white vase that I'm hoping she'll get bored of one day...

The most important thing is, if you don't have the space and you don't use it, or you haven't used it in a long time... then get rid of it.

I've got one big exception to that rule: if something has got sentimental value, I don't get rid of it. Instead, I've made memory boxes for me and all the boys and Joe – I covered them in wrapping paper and labelled them with our names. Zach's is quite a big one – an old present box – but as the oldest, he's got more stuff than his brothers because he's been around the longest. (And Joe's is just a file that stands up!) Usually, I'll make sure the things I'm crafting have a theme, but I didn't make all the boxes at the same time so I don't mind that they don't match. It almost feels like they are memories in themselves. When the boys grow up and eventually move out, they can get rid of it all if they really want to. But I hope they'll want to keep their memories and be glad that I saved them all.

WHAT TO PUT IN A MEMORY BOX

It's all about what reminds you of happy times, or adventures you've been on. For me, it's about drawings that the boys have done (only the decent ones), their hospital stuff from when they were born, tickets to movies they've been to. Or, if we go to the beach or woods, they'll pick up sticks and stones – and obviously I can't just have a load of sticks and stones around the house! They just go in their memory boxes, too. I don't keep all of their birthday cards – so I'm doing a *bit* of sorting as I go along – but for special birthdays like Rex's first and Zach's thirteenth, I will keep those.

♡ Getting Into The Tap to Tidy Routine ♡

You might be wondering when I'm doing all this – when I find the time for my organising, crafts and other projects. So, here's how I find it works for me.

If I'm at home on a weekday, the boys would usually be at school. I get up, do my regular morning routine – I'll tell you all about that in a minute – and then the kids will go to school. Since having Rex, I'd wait until his morning naptime to do something for myself. Whether that be a little craft or organising a cupboard, or getting up to date with paperwork or the washing or whatever, I really like to use his naps as time for me. (I would love to be one of those people that can just nap when the baby does, but I just end up lying there thinking, come on! Sleep!) When he's bit older (and not napping), it might be about finding time when he's playing. Likewise, you could be working, or studying, or home with kids, but it's all about looking for those little pockets of time in your day to make the most of them.

And don't be afraid to start small. It doesn't have to be a big old job like sorting out the garage – I might just be organising my candle drawer (by colours, then sizes). But if I can do a few jobs like that, that might take me twenty-five minutes, half an hour each, I am so satisfied. I like to have some kind of structure, and that's how I build it into my day.

MAKING WORK WORK

My days are totally different if I'm off to work on *Loose Women* – usually on Thursdays and Fridays. I'll try to make a quick, easy breakfast for the boys, get myself ready and then go. I can actually get quite sad when I'm working because I feel like they don't see me all day. But if I make breakfast, I've had a moment with them – we've done something together. And then I'll go to the studio, rehearse, do the show, have a debrief, come back home. Usually it'll be a pickup before 7am and I'll get home for about four o'clock in the afternoon.

Then, the boys will normally want an animal snack – just fruit or veg that I'll make into the shape of an animal (or a dinosaur, or a desert island... I have so much fun). So I make them a little snack, and that makes me feel good as well. Sometimes I don't – sometimes I get home and think, sod that, I can't be bothered! But often I'll make them a snack and then it's into dinner, bath-time and bedtime.

♡ Build Your Own ♡
Tap to Tidy Day

If you're the type of person that's a little bit like me and often feels quite tight-chested – my shoulders are kind of up by my ears half the time, as I worry about what I've got to do – you might find that a bit of structure to your day really works. A really loose structure – it has to be loose, and you have to be comfortable knowing that, if something doesn't happen, it really doesn't matter. But if you've got little points to look forward to during the day, it can distract your mind from going off into dark places and help you to have a happier time.

It's not rigid, and it's not guaranteed. If I don't get lots done, I don't beat myself up. But, if I can hit certain points, then I feel like I've had an organised day. Even if I just:

♡ Make my bed.

♡ Make some sort of food or a fun snack for the boys.

♡ Have some me time with crafting or organising.

Then I feel like that is a good day for me!

QUICK BED TIDY

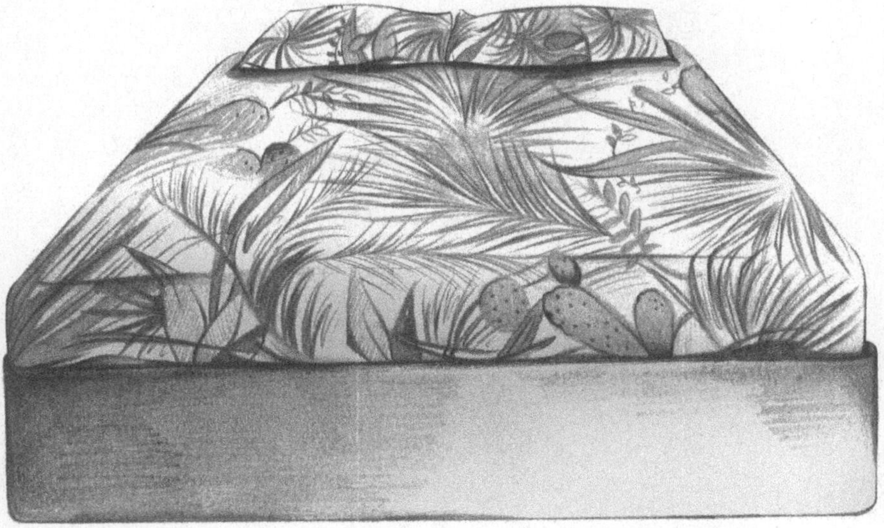

Done ✓

Snack Time

ORANGE DOG

I love making the boys' fruit or veg snacks look like something that will make them smile! (I've even arranged Joe's takeaway to look like a panda on the plate... the rice is its white bits, of course!) This really easy dog takes just an orange and a few blueberries to do.

One orange
Four blueberries

1. Cut three round slices from the orange – one for the body, then one each for the head and muzzle/nose.

2. Cut a couple of orange wedges for ears, and a few smaller slices for the legs and tail.

3. Give him a blueberry nose and two eyes – and cut a blueberry in half to give him little eyebrows, too.

Orange slices

Give him some features!

Done ✔

Snack Time

ALL-DAY BREAKFAST BAKE

I'll shove anything in a pastry! But this is one of my favourites.

Puff pastry
Grated cheese
Two or three eggs
Half a dozen bacon rashers

1. Just fold over the edges of some puff pastry to give it a rim (I use a full sheet) and transfer to a baking tray.

2. Sprinkle with a handful of grated cheese, crack in two or three eggs, throw in six or seven rashers of bacon, and you're away.

3. Chuck it in the oven for 20 minutes at 180 degrees C (the first time you make it, see how it's doing in your oven: sometimes it's done in mine in just 10–15 minutes). It's so easy and I can pick at that all day – it's like a fry-up in a pastry, it's so good!

P.S. I do a similar thing with Marmite and cheese: roll out a sheet of puff pastry, cover it in Marmite, some grated cheese, then roll it back up again into a log. Cut it into slices, pop these on a baking tray and put it in the oven at 180 degrees C, for about 15–20 minutes. In Australia, they're called Vegemite scrolls, but I do mine with Marmite, so they're Marmite scrolls.

Sprinkle of
cheese

Crack on
the eggs

Throw on
the bacon

Bake!

Done ✔

Maybe you could tell yourself, I'd love to organise my wire drawer at some point, and then write next to it when that could be – if you finish work and don't have anything planned that evening, or, if you've got children, perhaps when Mum comes over and she's playing with the kids for a little while. You don't have to give yourself a strict time, but it means you will be thinking about those little, achievable things and when you could get them done – instead of the scary stuff that sometimes takes over.

♡ Why Everyone Needs ♡ A Bit Of Tap to Tidy

Even if you're not a worrier like me, you may find you really like a bit of structure to your day. Even Joe! I never thought he really cared much about routine: he's quite slapdash, he's not organised and he's sort of like a whirlwind! But actually, the pandemic really hit him hard because before, he would go to the gym almost every day, when the kids went to school. Not for long, but it was his one thing that he always did that he really appreciated. Not having that was really hard for him.

So I know that he does need a certain amount of routine to his day – he has to have some sort of goal. (Although our days still look very different. While I'd relax by organising or crafting, Joe would watch the telly – he loves *Forged in Fire*, a show about making swords. I can't bloomin' bear it. It is so boring! But that's how *he* zones out – he watches people build swords!)

AND WHEN IT'S ALL GOING WRONG

So, you've got your list for the day of little things you'd like to get done. And then it all goes off the rails.

It happens to me all the time. Sometimes Rex's just like, not today, Mummy. I'm not going to eat any of your breakfast. I'm going to throw it all over the floor and up the walls. I don't fancy getting dressed either and if you don't carry me all day, I will scream. On those days, I just admit defeat. There's no point fighting it or beating myself up about the things I haven't managed to achieve. I just have to say, well done for getting through those moments. That in itself is an achievement.

When your day ends up like this, throw the list out the window and do what really matters to you – the rest can wait.

If there is one thing I try to do every day, it's make the bed. I hate getting into it unmade. It just makes me feel gross. But sometimes I get up so early that Joe's still asleep in it. And then the day begins, everyone gets up, and I'm busy with other things.

So, I'll just do it later – even if I'm making the bed at five o'clock. (And if you're wondering how often I change the sheets, it's once a week, max – unless something happened in there… *you* know. But not much is happening in there!)

And in the meantime, I just focus on the little things that make me happy.

♡ Making Memories Every Day ♡

I love making memories. It doesn't have to be something big, some over-the-top holiday or anything like that. Even just going for a walk in the woods with the kids, or going out into the garden and digging with them – I love that so much. I just love being around the boys, if I'm honest with you. And if I craft something connected to that memory, it will be so special to me. For example, I made a stone family from some pebbles that we collected on holiday. Every time I look at it, it just reminds me of how happy we were when we were there. I'm in love with it!

Make Up

YOUR STONE FAMILY (OR FRIENDS)

I'm always looking at crafting ideas online, so I'd seen people arrange pebbles in a frame to make a little stone family, labelled 'Mum', 'Dad' and so on. I didn't know if I wanted to make another frame to hang up, because we do have a lot around the house. Instead, I got a big pebble and thought, I'll stand us all up on this.

Pebbles
Candle (optional)

1. I found some body-sized pebbles and some little round pebbles for our heads. That's it!

2. I just glued them all on top of each other using the big pebble as a base – and stuck a candle on there, too, so it could be functional as well.

Finish with a candle

Bit of glue!

Done ✓

♥ ♥
♥ *Tip* Glue (I use a glue gun, as it really holds things together) and scissors are pretty much essential for crafting, so I won't include either of them in the list of things you need for make ups.

In fact, that seems the perfect moment to share my go-to list of what I use again and again around the house.

TAP TO TIDY TOP TEN – MY HOUSEHOLD HEROES!

1. Tension rods. I've got these adjustable rods everywhere.

2. Curtain clips. The little rings, or hooks, with clips attached, that you'd use to hang up a shower curtain. But I'm just as likely to use them to arrange my crisp packets!

3. A glue gun. This pumps out proper heavy-duty glue to stick things together when the usual stuff just won't cut it.

4. Sticky hooks. I hang up almost everything with stick-on hooks (the brand I use is Command) that you can put pretty much anywhere, with no need for nails.

5. Good scissors. Which means sturdy and sharp. There's nothing worse than a blunt pair!

6. A decent drill. Mine has loads of different attachments and it was only a cheap one from IKEA. Just make sure it has the drill bits that mean you can drill wood and glass, too, as you get more confident with it – so you can drill anything, basically!

7. A ball of string. Everything looks nicer if you wrap it in string! You can take an empty wine bottle, wrap it in string to make it look pretty, and I've seen that sold in the shops for a fiver. I use brown, rustic-looking string, labelled 'natural twine'.

8. Candles and wax melts. They make me feel homely.

9. Fake flowers. They make everything look nice and last forever.

10. Spray paint. If you ever want to change something quickly, spray paint is the way to go. It's cheap and easy and has maximum effect. P.S. Don't forget, always use a spray primer first and a sealer to keep the paint looking fresh.

Right, let's start the day.

Good Morning!

I'm an early riser, not by choice but because I had kids so young I've never really been able to lie in – not since I was eighteen anyway!

Still, the best thing that I can possibly do to make the most of my morning is go to bed early. If I go to bed between nine and ten o'clock, then I wake up about six without an alarm, which is an hour before I need to wake any of the kids for school. It just gives me that hour so I'm not shot out of bed thinking, sugar, I've got to get everything done in ten minutes and go!

♡ Tapping Into Your Golden Hour ♡

If I'm awake at six o'clock and no one else is up, then I do feel like that is my golden hour. If the first thing I get to do when I wake up is be alone, that is goals! I love it when that happens. Sometimes Rex's up at that time. Sometimes everyone's up at that time. But sometimes I get it all to myself. I'm not often on my own with three kids – four kids, when Joe's Harry is with us, too – so there's something really special about that.

Don't get me wrong, I love and live for my children, but I am not ashamed to say that having a moment alone is fundamental to my mental health.

I don't like to just jump straight out of bed. That is not me. I like to lie there for a good twenty minutes and just enjoy my bed and the silence for a little while. I might go through emails on my phone, see what work I've got coming up, or research things that I want to do in the house.

♡ My Happy ♡
Thoughts Jar

Some mornings I wake up a little anxious, wondering, am I going to get everything done, am I doing enough for the kids? I don't know, silly things. I just worry. So when I wake up like that, I get the notepad I keep by my bed and draw a jar.

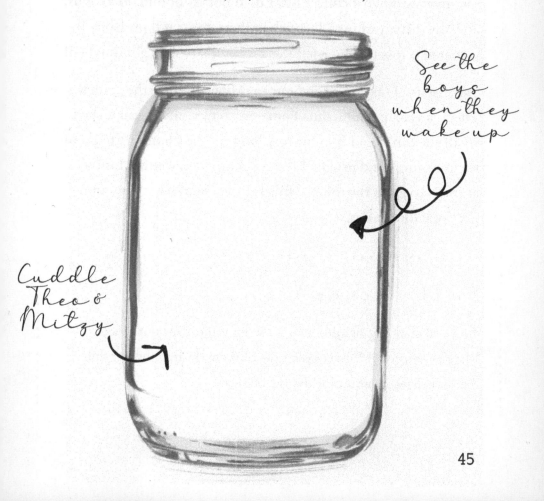

See the boys when they wake up

Cuddle Theo & Mitzy

I write nice things inside it, just positive thoughts – little things I'm really grateful for, or excited about, and that make me happy. I'll lay there for a bit, until my dog Theo's like, come on, Mum, I'm going to wet myself!

My Morning Montage

Once I'm up, the first thing I need to do is let the animals out. On my way down, I collect Rex's used bottles of milk in a caddy, and any dirty washing I'll chuck in there, too – it'll probably be scattered across the floor, left there when everyone's got into bed!

Downstairs, I take Theo and our cat Mitzy out into the garden – Theo's a teacup Chihuahua Pomeranian mix, and because she's small she can't hold it in for very long. So she's bursting to go in the morning! And usually I'll sit in the garden waiting for the animals to go to the toilet, while I think about what I've got to get done for the day.

Little things I love

I love to stalk my neighbour's roses hanging over our fence. They're so pretty! I'll take pictures of them on my phone while I'm out there, waiting for the fur babies.

Then, I will come back inside and make myself a cup of tea: builder's, milk, two sugars. I'm not a lemon and water girl – I wish I was! And I'll probably chuck the washing in the laundry baskets in the utility room (more on that in a bit) and put a load on – that way I stay on top of it. Then, if no one else is up, I will just get started on a task. Sometimes I find morning's the easiest time to get things done because I get a few moments to myself, which I really enjoy. I might make a breakfast for the kids ready for when they wake up, so I haven't got to do anything later on.

Here are two of the easiest breakfasts I do.

Breakfast Time

CREAM CHEESE OAT TART

Base mix: Two cups of oats to a quarter cup of honey, plus a couple of tablespoons of flaxseed (banana: optional)
Cream cheese for the topping
Your favourite fruit

1. Mix the oats, honey and flaxseed for the base. I've given the rough proportions above, which you can tweak depending on how much you want to make/how hungry you are! If you think it's not going to stick together (you want it a bit sticky), you can always throw in a mashed-up banana.

2. Squash it into a pie dish or paper case. Use the back of a spoon to really pack it down. I put mine in a giant paper cupcake case, because I find it easier to get it out, but you could put it into little cupcake cases to make mini ones, or just leave it in the pie dish.

3. Let that harden in the fridge for about 20 minutes. If you're worried that your fridge isn't cold enough, shove it in the freezer – it won't hurt it. You could even put it in the fridge the night before, if you want to make this for the next morning.

48

4. Spread the base with cream cheese. I'll use a whole tub! Sometimes I mix it with honey so it's a bit sweeter.

5. Top it with your favourite fruit: strawberries, blueberries, anything really!

Most of the time I like to make more of this than I need, because then I don't have to make breakfast every day. It can also be a nice dessert for the kids.

If I'm feeling *really* energetic, then I'll make a big stack of pancakes (see page 50).

Bit of fruit

Shape in a cupcake case

Cream cheese

Done ✓

Breakfast Time

LION PANCAKES

Pancake batter
Oil or butter, for greasing
Tangerines, broken into segments
Chocolate syrup or black icing pen

1. Use whatever pancake recipe you like! I just mix flour, milk and eggs in a bowl and wait for it to get to the texture that looks like pancake batter! (But 100g plain flour, two large eggs and 300ml milk will make about six pancakes, if you want to measure it out.)

2. Pour some of the batter into a greased pan on a medium heat and cook the pancakes on each side for about a minute. Do them one at a time, and you can keep them warm in the oven on the lowest heat as you make them.

3. Put one on a plate, arrange tangerine segments around the top to make a mane. Finish by drawing on a smiley face with a little nose and whiskers in chocolate syrup or black icing.

P.S. Instead of pancakes, you can also use porridge. Put the porridge in a bowl, arrange tangerine segments around the edge for the mane, and finish it off with syrup or icing.

After that, I've probably got fifteen minutes to go, if it's a school day, before I need to make sure the boys are up. I will check their school bags, make sure that they've put everything in there, and sometimes get their lunch sandwiches done. Which brings me on to…

♡ A Message For The Parents! ♡

Sometimes we do things because we think they're the right thing to do, but they don't make us happy. At one point, I was doing *everything* for my kids, so they didn't have to do a thing. I thought that's what good mums do. And sometimes that would really bloomin' stress me.

For instance, I'd catch myself rowing with Zach about why he didn't have his tie on yet for school, and he'd say, 'It's in my blazer pocket – I'll put it on when I go out of the door!' And I thought, why am I arguing with my son about this? If he wants to go to school without his tie on and get his detention, he has to make that decision for himself.

I realised it was all about control (again!). The truth is I cannot control what the boys do when they go out that front door. I'm not going to be there to run after them every second of every day. So the best thing that I can do is to encourage them to look after themselves. That means I will check, say, that they've remembered their PE kit. But ultimately, as they get older, the responsibility is on them to make sure they're ready for school. If I'm working and not around in the morning, my two eldest can make themselves a packed lunch, they can make their own breakfast, and they can make sure that they're dressed appropriately and going to school with all the right equipment. Whether they do it or not is another story but, the bottom line is, on their heads be it.

And it makes my life easier because I'm sharing the burden a little bit. It took me a long time to realise how helpful that is, and also that other people can do things as well as I can. A lot of the time, we can think that no one can do it the way that we do it, so I'm just gonna do it myself. And actually, that's counterproductive. In my case, I was putting too much pressure on myself and also undermining my children. I was indirectly telling them that they were not good enough without even realising it! That's why, as time goes on, it makes me happier as a parent to let them do things for themselves.

So, that first hour of the day for me is just golden. It gives me a moment to myself to collect my thoughts.

Now, I'll be thinking, is everyone starting to wake up? If not, I will get the boys out of their beds and in the shower, and I might get my shower in then and get dressed, but to be honest, most of the time I don't manage to get dressed and washed until after the school run. I won't bother with makeup. I *need* my eyelashes on – most of the time, I sleep in them and sometimes I'll glue the corners back down! – but aside from that, I don't really put on any makeup if I'm not going anywhere. I might put moisturiser on, or if family's coming over maybe some highlighter, so I don't look so tired. But outside of that I can't be bothered. I really enjoy doing my makeup if I've got loads of time. I don't enjoy it if I have to rush it!

Tidy

YOUR COSMETICS COLLECTION

(OR, MY MAKEUP BAKING TRICK... AND YES, I MEAN PROPER BAKING!)

I think I have a lot of makeup. But then I see other people's collections… and I'm like, OK, I don't have a lot! Honestly, it tends to be just whatever I've used forever and ever. I'll experiment more with skincare, because I feel a bit braver with that, whereas I feel with makeup it's easy to mess it up: if you don't get what's right, everyone can immediately see!

53

But I do like to know what I've got. In my makeup drawer, I used to have drawer organisers – little tubs – that were getting on my nerves because I couldn't really see what was inside them. At the same time, I had so many shelves in my oven that it was annoying me: every time I wanted to put something in there I had to move all these metal grilles around. I took them out and thought, I could put them inside my drawer and stack my makeup. So I did!

I laid two oven shelves flat inside my makeup drawer, then arranged my makeup between the wires, so it couldn't roll around. It looks smart – you can't see the oven shelves – and helps me keep my makeup arranged by type: lips, face, whatever.

MY SEVEN MAKEUP STAPLES

1. False eyelashes – usually from Doll Beauty.

2. Duo Quick-Set eyelash glue – I use that on all my lashes, because it doesn't smell like fish (like a lot of the others do!).

3. MAC Studio Fix Fluid Foundation – my colour is NW20 and I get the same one every single time. I just can't find another one that works like that on my skin.

4. There's a Smashbox palette called Cali Contour that I use over my whole face. So it's my eyeshadow, my eyebrows and my contour and my highlighter.

5. Lip gloss – I've got a Huda Beauty one that I like.

6. Mascara – any of the Maybelline ones because they've got really fat fluffy brushes that I love. And yes, I do put it on top of my false lashes.

7. Tanner – I've used Dove Gradual Tan for years. It's the only tanner that I can use where I don't get streak marks. I get the medium to dark shade, rub it in like a moisturiser after my shower and I never get a streak. I just gradually get slightly browner. (I do still give my hands a good scrub so I don't get stains.)

And if something works, then I'll keep it. If my mascara says it's out of date but it still goes on, I'm not throwing it away! Makeup's really expensive these days. If I've got makeup I don't use any more, then I will clear it out and give it to my nieces (I'll make them little gift bags) because they love it. Or if I have any cosmetics that I've not used and are still in date, I will donate them to an amazing charity called Beauty Banks (www.beautybanks.org.uk). But outside of that, I don't throw it away at all. And I would *never* get rid of a lovely perfume bottle! Let me tell you why…

Make Up

Turn Your Perfume Bottle Into A Fragrance Diffuser

This is what I call a make up, when I look at something and think, how can I *make this up* and maybe make it a bit better than what it is? I'll keep my used perfume bottles for years sometimes, before I make them up into something else. I don't tend to take the labels off, because I think they're really pretty. But I do need to remove the spray nozzle.

Protective gloves, if you have them
Pliers
Old perfume bottle
Little funnel
Diffuser refill oil and diffuser sticks

1. The trick is, wear a pair of protective gloves and get a pair of pliers – I use the ones in my toolkit.

2. Then, as you're looking at the perfume bottle, you'll see the piece of metal that clasps around the top of the glass bottle will sort of lip over the edges. Use the pliers to gently squeeze and lift up the metal lip, firmly but slowly working all the way around.

3. Then give it a little shake and it should just come off. I'll then put a little funnel in there, pour in some diffuser oil that I'll pick up in the shops, and then add some diffuser sticks. Or, if I feel like using it as a vase, I add a fake flower. Easy!

You can do a similar thing with any crusty old fragrance diffuser that's got all dried-up and yellow-looking. Just carefully pour in boiling water to get rid of any yellow staining, then refresh it with new diffuser oil and sticks. I also filled the bottom third of one of mine with little white pebbles from my garden and added a flower – a fake white rose. I love looking at it now: I think, I made that!

Tip Take the label off that old diffuser that's run out, clean it properly, add some stones and a fake flower and a new smell... and you'll love it again.

Pour in new oil

Add diffuser sticks

Done ✓

So the boys are in school, the Pickle (Rex!) is dressed, I'm dressed – hopefully – and now it's time to make the bed.

MAKE THE BED (WITH MY SAVE YOUR NAILS HACK)

Joe doesn't like making the bed, and to be honest with you, I don't like him doing it either, because it's terrible when he does. I really like to get into a tight bed. I want to have to fight with my covers when I get into it! And I love to do this because it's so easy. Just pull everything off, smooth out the sheet, waft the duvet over, put two sleep pillows flat at the top and then stand the other two, pretty sleeping pillows at the front. Then tuck in the duvet. As I go along, I use an ordinary wooden hanger to tuck everything into the bed frame really tightly. Just use one end of the hanger to tuck the sheet, duvet or blanket right into the side of the bed, between the mattress and the frame, all the way around. I'll stretch that blanket out until it can't be stretched anymore and that's why my bedding looks smooth, like it's been ironed. (But I don't iron my bedding. I hate ironing, so that would be my worst nightmare because bedding's so big.) My hanger hack means I don't hurt my hands. And I save my nails! I'll finish it all off with a spray of pillow spray.

Make Up

SCENTED PILLOW SPRAY

Distilled water
Witch hazel or vodka
Your favourite essential oils
Clean spray bottle

For my spray, I use 70ml of distilled water (posh bottled water), 20ml of witch hazel (you can use vodka as an alternative, if you've got it!) and 40 drops of essential oil – I use clary sage and bergamot, my two favourites. Then I might chuck in a few sprigs of dried lavender. Shake to mix, then spray. It's lovely!

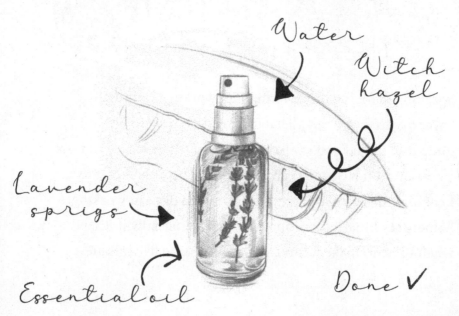

Water

Witch hazel

Lavender sprigs

Essential oil

Done ✓

Meanwhile, the boys will be asking, Where's my homework? Where's this, where's that? So I'll be looking for things, helping get them ready for school. Now he's at secondary school, Zach gets the bus, while I walk Leighton round to his school with Rex. After that, back home is when I feel, *right*. That's me. I've done the morning now, where's my tea? And I'll usually have another cup with some toast. People laugh at me, because I don't put butter on my toast. It's not that I don't like butter, it's just years of not having time. It would take two seconds more, but I feel I've saved so much time by skipping that and squeezing on some Marmite! Or, I'll have a slice of whatever I've made for the boys.

♡ How I Speed Up My Morning Routine ♡

Speaking of saving time… when I'm working, I normally have to leave quite early. That is when I do have to be a bit more disciplined and say to myself, if I want to make the boys a breakfast I'll have to set an alarm to get up at half-past five. I couldn't make anything extravagant on a day I'm working. Sometimes I make them apple donuts – especially if it's a Friday, when I like to make it fun – as they only take five minutes.

Breakfast Time

APPLE DONUTS

Apple (say, one per person)
Cream cheese
A fun topping – grated chocolate, honey, sugar sprinkles

If you cut out the core and then slice the apple horizontally, each slice has a little hole – that's your 'donut'. Spread cream cheese over each apple slice, then grate a bit of dark or milk chocolate on there or drizzle a bit of honey or something nice over it. And that's it! If I'm feeling really jazzy and the boys've been good, then I'll put some actual sprinkles on there.

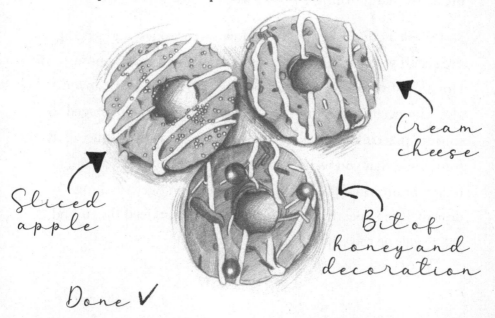

Cream cheese

Sliced apple

Bit of honey and decoration

Done ✓

♡ Time To Pat Yourself ♡ On The Back

(WHATEVER HAPPENS!)

Things go wrong all the time. Sometimes I'll wake up and everything's planned in my head and it just doesn't happen. Rex might be up at five o'clock and won't go back to sleep. Then the boys might have a meltdown before school because they've lost something. The other day I tried to make the breakfast oat tart and didn't leave it long enough in the fridge to set so it fell apart. Just accept defeat and tell yourself, it's not happening today! (The boys had special 'crumbled oats' for breakfast that morning…)

So I think a good morning boils down to breakfast and getting dressed. If you get other stuff done as well, then that's a bonus. Honestly, if you're fed, dressed, out the door, along with anyone else who needs to be, you've done a great job. If you managed to squeeze in a coffee or tea… bonus. If you managed to squeeze in something that you wanted to get done that day, that's an even bigger bonus! In all honesty, I sometimes don't get anything done before I take the kids to school other than feed them. And yes, I've done the school run in my pyjamas!

♡ *Hero Task* ♡
GET YOUR SH♥T TOGETHER IN YOUR WARDROBE

Remember how I said we'd be tackling the bigger tidying tasks, too – the ones for when you've got a bit more time to spare? I'm gonna call them hero tasks – the ones that make you feel like a superhero! In other words, this is where to begin if you've got no idea where to begin: where to start with those rooms or places where you just think, I'm not gonna bother.

And the wardrobe is definitely one of those places for me.

THE TRUTH ABOUT MY SHOPPING HABIT

I love going shopping. I online-shop a lot, but most of the time I just end up going into Primark – especially for the kids. They grow out of everything in seconds. Then for myself, it's really just as and when. So if I'm out and about and I see something in a charity shop, or in Primark, or wherever, then I'll grab it if I love it. And I will online-shop if I really need something – if I've run out of this or need some more of that.

The problem is, I find it really difficult to get rid of clothes. I just think, I *might* wear that one day… so my wardrobe can get out of control. However, I have got much better at deciding – if I haven't worn something in the last year or if I can't remember the last time I wore it, then I have to give it away because I'm not getting the use out of it. With clothes, I do think if an item's gone through every season of the year and you still haven't worn it, then someone else deserves it.

♥ ♥

♥ *Tip* I find that the more space I have, the more I'll fill it. So, a lot of people use the space-saving velvety hangers. But I actually prefer my hangers to be chunky – mostly white, wooden ones – because it gives me less space to just keep collecting clothes and makes me a bit more vigilant about getting rid of stuff. If there's a bit of a gap between each garment, it just feels a bit clearer in my head – if that makes sense! (Although if you've got a small wardrobe and you're trying to save space, those thin velvet hangers are the way to go, because they're small and non-slip.)

WHERE TO START WITH WARDROBE CHAOS

Sometimes I just shove things in drawers, because I can't be bothered to hang them back up on the hanger. Sometimes I just won't put things back in the right place. Then I will see my wardrobe and think, this is a disaster, I don't know where anything is! And it makes me feel like I haven't got any clothes. I'll just go and get something out of my clean washing basket!

When it gets like that I have to just get it all out, as I would when I Tap to Tidy anything.

But – and this is a big 'but' here… the way that I organise my wardrobe is a really slow process. It's not slapdash. So I will take it out *section by section*. I'll start with my underwear, for example. I take it all out of the drawer, spread it across the floor and just actually look at it. Because what I've noticed with clothes is that I end up gravitating towards exactly the same thing every day! I have all this stuff that never gets worn because I just want to wear the same things over and over again. With my underwear, there might be three pairs of granny pants that I wear that just circulate in and out of the wash. I love them and they're comfy and that's what I want to wear. So, I will pick out those things – the ones I go for every day – and I'll put them in my Definitely Keeping pile.

Once I've found a home for those (more on my system for *that* in a second), I'll look through the remaining pile of stuff that I've been ignoring: the Maybes. And I'll say, am I ever actually going to wear this? Is this thong comfortable? No, that's why I've never picked it out. Do I like this matching set? And I'll just get rid of anything I know, deep down, that I'm not going to wear. If it's been sitting in there for ages and I've not worn it, then it's just got to go.

And then you keep going, section by section. Take every single thing out, lay it out, and look at it for a little while. Do I wear it? Do I love it? Do I need it? Do I want to keep it? Is it worth me keeping it? As you're doing that, put aside the things that you're definitely going to keep.

With the rest, instead of dividing it into Bin It or Recycle piles, the first thing I'll do is say to my mum, my sister, Joe's sisters, do you want anything? They'll have a rummage and if they don't want it, it'll go straight to charity. I find some charity shops don't accept clothes, or certain items, because they've got too much. I try to find the places that really need them and get it to them. There's a really good charity that collects bras (www.smallsforall.org), so I end up donating to them, for example.

WHY I COLOUR-CODE MY CLOTHES

I like to hang up my clothes by colour. So instead of grouping together my dresses, shirts, whatever, everything is organised by shade: white, black, pink. That works for me, because most of the time, I'll just look and think, what colour do I want to wear today? I know that sounds really weird, but I'll feel a bit beige, or a bit black, and then I just go to that section (and end up probably picking out a lounge set).

If you want to try it, just sort your Definitely Keeping pile by colours before you put it all back. Then, tackle one colour at a time. Put your whites back in first – hang the white dresses next to each other, then white shirts, white jumpers, white trousers – then go on to the next colour. By the time you're done, everything's colour-coordinated, and each colour section is coordinated by garments, too. It's so satisfying.

SORT YOUR DRAWERS

My system's a bit different in my drawers: they are colour-coordinated, but first I group everything by what it is – it just makes it easier to find things. So, my top drawer is jeans and jeggings, arranged so they go from black to dark to light to white. The next drawer down is gym stuff – leggings on one side, sports bras on the other. It's the drawer that never gets opened, I'm not gonna lie! Then I've got a drawer for two-piece matching tracksuits and lounge sets, and another for swimming costumes and bikinis, and they're all in colour order, too.

On the opposite side of my dressing room, my top drawer is for jewellery – I don't use a jewellery box because I forget what I've got. Instead, I spread it out in a drawer and use a lot of little things to keep everything in place: ring holders, necklace holders, bracelet holders, and little plastic tubs with compartments. Underneath that are my accessories – hats, belts, sunglasses – all in fabric boxes (I use IKEA ones) to keep them tidy.

Next is underwear: bras on one side, knickers on the other, in little fabric boxes as well. I also divide my knickers by type, so I have comfy old period knickers for when I'm on, knickers for dressing up – if I need a thong so I don't have a knicker line, I mean! – and my favourite everyday ones, which are just seamless, ugly beige knickers that I bloomin' love. I buy mine from a place called Freya Lingerie, they're the best ones I've found so far, and believe me, I've tried a few. My bras are the same: I have the nice ones I never wear, and sporty crop-top bras that I live in. And I've some nursing bras as well, just in case I get pregnant again! The drawer down from that is pyjamas, and I've also got a drawer of odds and sods: sarongs or random gilets. That's handy for all your stuff that doesn't really have a home – when you don't know what it is!

♥ ♥

♥ Tip To display my shoes, I've fixed tension rods – those adjustable rods you can shove pretty much anywhere – in a space between a cabinet and a wall. Then I hang shower curtain rings off the horizontal rods, using the little clips designed for the curtain to clip onto my shoes and hang them up! It keeps them really tidy and visible.

Little things I love: **Dressing comfy!**

My go-to outfit is a lounge set and slippers. I get my sets from In The Style, Primark, and eBay. Often I'll just search online for whatever material or colour I fancy – for a 'cable-knit lounge set' or 'pastel lounge set'. A designer called Olivia Rubin made a tracksuit that looked like she'd woven it while sitting on a rainbow. She was donating some of the profits of the sales to charities for frontline key workers, so even though it was expensive, I bought it! And I wear slippers because I think, why the hell would anyone want to wear their shoes in the house?! The insides *have* to be fluffy!

DON'T FORGET THE SEASONAL SWAP OUT

I will do a big swap out twice a year. If we're going into autumn/ winter, I will take all of my summer stuff out and put it in vacuum bags; and I'll do the same with my heavier clothes when the weather starts warming up. And I'll use those moments to have a tidy, too: spread it all out across the floor, work out what I loved wearing. Anything that I didn't wear will go, and anything that I loved wearing will be put into a vacuum bag that I keep underneath our bed. Our bed opens up with storage in it and it's an absolute lifesaver for season swaps.

Time For Me ♡

There are two adults in our house and thankfully, although Joe's day certainly starts out slower than mine, by the time I get back from the school run, he's picked up where I left off.

He's washing up the breakfast things, hoovering and generally just helping. And, quite frankly, he'd better be because it would be difficult to swallow, waking up and letting him have a lie-in and then coming home to him still being in bed.

I'm really lucky with Joe, he does most of the hoovering and mopping, they're his favourite of all the chores. I call them the fun ones. I'll do a big deep clean once or twice a week, but Joe will hoover every day. Sometimes twice a day, because when you've got kids, cats and dogs, you're lucky if you only have to hoover twice a day.

Tip Just because something needs to be done, doesn't mean it can't be enjoyable. Sometimes if the older boys go to their dads', or if they're out doing something else and the house is clear, then I like to put the music on really loud and have a dance and a sing while I'm on my feet with the Hoover and mop. Honestly, that is one of my favourite things to do.

While Joe's doing the fun chores, I'll sort out the washing I put on earlier in the morning.

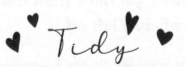

Sort The Washing (No Ironing Involved)

I've got a couple of systems that really will make things easier.

When I made over my utility room (more on that in a moment), I bought three big swing bins designed for rubbish and spray painted them pink, and now they are my laundry bins. I decided that one would be for lights, one for whites and one for darks. It means there's now a proper system in my utility, rather than one overflowing washing basket that means you have to separate all your colours. And, if you take away the laundry bins upstairs it forces everybody to bring their dirty clothes down to the utility room. It's a bit of a game for the boys now: they'll put their clothes in the right baskets and they know exactly what to do and there are no excuses about not knowing where to put the washing. I never have to separate a load these days – this system really does work.

♥ ♥
♥ *Tip* Get three laundry bins, or one with three compartments, then make sure you put them near wherever you actually do the laundry.

When the clothes come out, they will either go in the tumble dryer or be hung up on the rail attached to my utility ceiling. I actually don't like hanging things on there anymore because the clothes cover all the pink prettiness! But it is very useful.

♥ ♥
♥ *Tip* When you take your clean clothes out of the machine, any items that hang in your cupboards, put them on hangers straight away, then put them on the washing line so that when they're dry, they are so much easier to put away and it's less daunting than having a huge pile of clean, folded washing.

I've got some crocheted baskets in the utility – one is for me and Rex, then there's one each for the older boys. I'll fold up the washing, put it in the right basket, and then the boys when they're home have to take their basket and put it away. As for Joe, he does his own.

I can't bear ironing – you get one shirt done in the time it would take to clean the whole house! So I try to buy stuff for me and the kids that you don't have to iron. I've also got a handheld steamer that I use if worst comes to worst and I have to iron something (the boys' school shirts, or if I am going out and I'll be embarrassed if I don't!). But Joe loves to iron. He irons every day – a right weirdo! His clothes won't look creased at all and he'll say they're disgusting, he's got to iron them. Well, alright then Bubs, you go for it. While you're there can you do the kids' school shirts?!

And while we're talking about Joe…

Scrabble letters

Lego

Done ✓

74

Make Up

FATHER'S DAY LEGO FRAME

Joe loves this one. We made it for him for Father's Day.

Lego family (pick figures to reflect your family or friends)
Photo frame with a couple of centimetres depth (so Lego
   figures can fit underneath the glass or plastic)
Scrabble letters (spelling out your chosen message)

1. The hardest part of this is tracking down the Lego figures
    to match your family or friends!

2. Once you've got them, start by undoing the frame and
    taking out the paper or card inside that's going to be
    your background.

3. Glue the figures onto the paper in a line, and above them
    glue Scrabble letters to spell out your message. I did 'Never
    Lego' (Never Let Go!).

4. Then you just write the names under each figure (in pencil
    first to make sure you're happy) and put it all back inside
    the frame.

Make Up

JOE'S FAVOURITE PHOTO FRAME

With a lot of my make ups, Joe will be like, oh my G-d, what the hell is this – do we have to have them everywhere?! He's just teasing, but this is one thing I made he actually really liked!

Two sticks, about the same length
String (see the list on page 41 for my favourite)
Fake foliage (don't spend much – I buy mine from eBay usually)
Mini fairy lights (if they've a battery attached you won't have
*   to plug them in)*
Mini wooden pegs or clips
Photos

1. Your sticks are going to be the top and bottom of your 'frame'.

2. Tie four pieces of string of equal length to one stick, then tie the other end of each string to the second stick, so they hang straight down.

3. Next, tie one more piece of string to the top stick, attaching it at each end – this is what you'll use to hang it from a nail or hook on the wall.

4. Wrap some fake foliage and fairy lights around the sticks to decorate them, then peg photos to the vertical strings: I just printed off some of us as a family.

Bit of foliage

Sticks

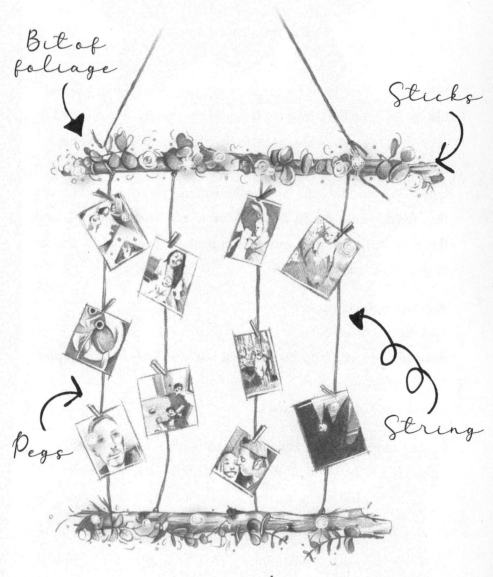

Pegs

String

Done ✔

Snack Time

CHOCOLATE PENCILS

When I put Rex down for his morning nap, that's when I would like to do something for myself: something crafty. Sometimes I'll prep the after-school snack, because when the boys get home they're bloomin' starving. They act as though they've never eaten before in their life! And they really demand my attention because they haven't seen me all day, so I like to not be distracted. I made this for them when they were going back to school, and I wanted to give them something fun.

A bar of white chocolate
Pink food colouring
Basically, use any long biscuits that you can find. I used sponge
    finger/trifle biscuits
Chocolate chips (milk or dark)

1. Break up the white chocolate and divide it between two heatproof bowls, then melt it (either in a bowl over a pan of simmering water, stirring, or pop it in the microwave – stirring it every 20 seconds).

2. Once it's melted, mix a little pink colouring in one bowl and leave the other one white.

3. Take each biscuit and dip either end in each colour of chocolate – so you've got the pink end as the pencil rubber and the white end as the nib.

4. Put a little chocolate chip on the nib to look like the lead of the pencil. And that's it! Leave the biscuits to cool and set. It's really easy, but I love them.

♥ ♥

♥ *Tip* Sometimes, if I've got a bit of time, I will prep a snack in advance, but leave a bit undone so the kids can help me later, if they want. So with the chocolate pencils, I'd break up all the chocolate, put it into bowls, get the biscuits out, get the chocolate chips out, and then probably melt the chocolate just before I leave to go and pick up Leighton (as it only takes me 10 minutes). That way, the kids can get stuck in and finish it off, but I can give them my full attention after school.

♡ How I Handle ♡ Life Admin

(OR, MAKING PLANS WHEN YOU CAN'T PLAN)

If I need to head out to do some food shopping, I'll do that in the morning, too. When Rex wakes up, it's a bit of stimulation for him and also something for me to enjoy! I very rarely do an online food shop. I find when I do, I miss things out and buy stuff that we don't actually need. Whereas when I go into the supermarket I'll see things and think, I forgot I needed that. I genuinely enjoy walking around – it's a day out for me!

When I share my shopping trips, I often get complaints about how boring it must get for Rex going to the supermarket. Let me just tell you, the kids love it. And even if they don't, tough luck, because they're either coming shopping with us or there's no food in the house, so we may as well make a day of it. So don't feel guilty about it. In my opinion, it's 1) sensory (bright colours, lights, different faces, different smells), 2) educational (learning life skills, seeing different food groups, as they get older counting – adding and subtracting), 3) sociable (meeting new people, interacting), 4) fun… for me at least. I love a good food shop.

Life admin is very much a day-to-day thing for me, on an 'as and when' basis. The truth is, I can't plan much ahead, even if I wanted to. My and Joe's work just doesn't allow for it because jobs can be very last-minute and everything can change at once. If I were to book a holiday for Christmas, and then a life-changing job came in, I would have to cancel that holiday. I've come to accept the fact that if we're going to do something, we have to do it there and then, or I just have to say, right, tomorrow we're doing this!

Dealing With What We Can't Control

I think that uncertainty's partly why I love to organise the little things inside my home. A lot of my life is out of my control and we fear things we can't control – that's why I sometimes get scared about dying, and things like that. So, having some kind of control in my home is a massive help with that.

Of course, any one of us can feel out of control – and recently, a lot of us have felt that more than usual: not being able to plan ahead, or book a holiday, or know what we were doing for Christmas, on top of everything else. But we *can* control the little things to make us happy in our own homes.

WHY I WRITE EVERYTHING DOWN

Once I do arrange something – even if it's just the vet the next day – I write it down in my diary. I find it really useful because I can forget things within ten minutes. I can book appointments and it's almost as if, because my brain knows I've done it, it wipes it away! I forget that I've even booked something.

When I put pen to paper, it sinks in a little bit more. And I felt that way all through school. Even if the teachers gave us a worksheet with everything we needed to know, I would have to copy that worksheet and write it down myself. Just thinking something doesn't put it into my brain. But when I have to think about the written words, it really reinforces what it is that I'm trying to remember. That's the same with anything that I need to hold on to or retain – any information I need to remember, I need to write it down physically.

♥ ♥

Tip I really struggle remembering people's names. The only thing that's helped with this over the years is to stop myself and listen to a name, then write it down somewhere later – most likely in the notebook I keep by my bed. It really helps. Also, I have to stop worrying about what I'm going to say next, as that often prohibits me listening to what the person is saying to me. In other words, listen. Really listen.

Time for a quick tidy.

Tidy

TACKLE A CUPBOARD

Sometimes I can think about certain cupboards for so long! The other day, I kept thinking about our snack cupboard because it was such a mess – and I had been contributing to that, just chucking stuff in there. In the kitchen, the snack cupboard gets messy the quickest, because everyone's in it all the time – it's like a vending machine. So when I did finally tidy it, my brain just felt like it had room around it. It was lovely.

If I need to clean a cupboard, I'll stick to my Tap to Tidy method. So, after facing up to the mess (I'd been thinking about that one for ages!), I will take everything out. Then I sort through what I've got into the piles: Bin It, Recycle (that'll be any empty packaging, say), Maybe, Definitely Keeping. I might also have a Give It Away pile.

Let's say I was doing the herbs and spices cupboard, where things can lurk for ages. I would check all the dates on my dried herbs, deciding which ones are going, which are maybe staying, and which are definitely staying. I might notice that I've got doubles of certain herbs: I'll see I've already got a coriander that I'm keeping. So can I pour one packet into the other? Or shall I just see if my mum wants some, because it's still usable?

I really try to think methodically about how I'm going to get things out of the cupboard again, so it doesn't get to the state that it was in when I first started. The key thing here is, if you can't see what's in the cupboard, it's never going to get used. And, if you're going to spend twenty hours looking for it, you'll just get frustrated. So, make sure that you can see it. You can still use all the space: if you've got those deep corner cupboards, for example, put your refills in the back. When I've run out of crisps or biscuits, I know exactly where the refills are – in that deep, dark nook of the cupboard, because I won't put anything in there that I need to use every day.

There are a few more little tips that help me organise things, depending on what's inside each cupboard…

MY SPICE SHELF HACK

Your cupboard shelves are normally held up by little metal pins and you can lower or raise them, depending on where you place the pins in the holes drilled inside the cupboard. So, I just took out two of the front pins of a shelf in my herbs and spices cupboard and left the back two where they were, so the shelf slanted down. Then, I put a tension rod at the front of the shelf, to act as a barrier. Now, my spices lie on that shelf at an angle, so I can see every single one instead of just rooting around hoping for the best. I take exactly what I want and put it straight back again. The cupboard itself might get slightly messy, because I might move some of the tins around that I keep in there. But those spices? Never! It's a much better system. Try it and see.

SHOW OFF YOUR SNACKS

It caused a bit of a fuss when I said on Insta that I hang up my crisp packets. But so many of you loved the idea! It keeps everything so neat and tidy. I use tension rods, which are great – their spring action keeps them in place, so you don't have to install any rod holders. Slide on some shower-curtain clips – the little metals hoops with a clip hanging off each one – before you put the rod in place, and clip them to anything you want to hang up. I hang up Rex's baby food pouches as well as my crisps. Underneath is a basket of treats, like Rolos. Then there's a big jar I chuck all my biscuits in, even ginger. Some visitors will say, urgh! But my kids still eat 'em! Happy days.

Tip I've struggled so much to recycle with three kids, because no one puts anything in the right bloomin' bin. The easiest way I found of dealing with that is by taking everything out of the packet (if it's something like a biscuit when it doesn't need to stay in its wrapper and can go straight in the jar). Then I can recycle the packaging immediately.

WHAT TO DO WITH AN UGLY MUG

My ugly mug box goes underneath the snacks – and it makes me laugh every time I look at it. I think some people must think I don't like the mugs they've given me, but they're actually my favourite ones! It's just that my mug cupboard has glass windows, and it would look so rubbish if I had all of my different-patterned mugs on show, because they're not uniform. So I put all of my posh white mugs in the glass-fronted cupboard and then I put the other mugs in a white plastic box from IKEA – really they're my sentimental mugs, the ones that actually mean something to me.

MAX YOUR PLATE SPACE

I like to use wooden plate racks: one side of our plate cupboard is for adult plates, one side is for Rex's things. On another shelf, I have tiered plate racks where our bowls and little plates go. Some of Rex's plastic plates have suction pads on the bottom and they don't all fit in there, so I stick them to the inside of the cupboard to keep them out of the way. (However, the suction wears off. So, just remember that they're gonna start falling off and scare the sh♥t out of you when you're sitting on the sofa!)

No More Smashed Glasses

Glasses have their own cupboard, with wine and champagne glasses at the bottom, tumblers on the next shelf, then jugs at the top. For my wine and champagne glasses, I ordered a wire rack from eBay. You screw it to the underneath of the shelf above (you just need a screwdriver) and slide your champagne and wine glasses in (upside down) by their bases, it's so handy. When they're freestanding in a cupboard somewhere, they always seem to break when you're trying to get one out. I find it much better to have them hanging in a rack.

Add A Secret Shelf

IKEA do something that I think is actual genius – a bracket that slides onto a shelf, so that you can have a little pullout container underneath it, in glass or plastic (look for their 365+ range). I've got one of them in the cupboard where Rex's plates are, and I put all his spoons and forks in there. And then I've got one in my pantry cupboard, and I put all my tealight candles in that. You could put one in your fridge as a pull-out drawer for chocolate or stuff that you don't really want the kids to see. Or, if you've got a cupboard for your paperwork, you could put one in for your pens and pencils. (I actually don't have a paperwork cupboard, much as I'd love to organise it – instead, I keep folders at my mum's because she helps me with my admin!)

CONTAIN THE MESS

Sometimes if I have things just loose in a cupboard, I'll fill the whole cupboard because I've got space for them – I'll just keep adding and adding, when I don't actually need that many products. If I'm using a container, it stops me falling into that trap. They're also great if you're dealing with things that shed little bits and pieces – baking decorations, for example – or if you need to take everything out easily. For example, having a container for all your everyday cleaning essentials means you can literally just take that box upstairs, not try to carry ten things through the house. But try to get containers that are not too high, so you can still see what's inside them. And there are certain places I wouldn't use them – I'd rather clip up my food packets, say, or stack my tins on a lazy Susan than have them in a container – again, it's about being able to see what you have.

♥ ♥
Tip When I'm buying any storage product, I would always ask myself, can I see what I've got in that? And just apply that rule every single time – because if you can't see what you've got, it doesn't do the job it's supposed to do!

♥ Hero Task ♥
OVERHAUL YOUR PANTRY

You might have noticed there's one cupboard I haven't mentioned. The biggest cupboard of 'em all! This is one for when you're feeling ready for a bit more of a challenge – the pantry.

In my kitchen, it's the really long cupboard next to the oven. On the bottom two drawers is baby-safe stuff, because whenever I open it, Rex is straight in there. So I'll just put bottles, dummies and all the stuff that he is allowed to play with, there. The next level is my baking stuff: baking tools, edible glitter and decorations. The layer above that is baking ingredients: flour and icing sugar, all of that. Above that is breakfast, so the boys can easily get to their cereals. And then just the next layer is nuts, seeds and pulses. So, it's *that* kind of cupboard.

It's also one that gets messy quite quickly because it's used all the time. I do a lot of baking and cooking, the boys are in there every day and Pickle (that's Rex, of course) plays at the bottom shelf all the bloomin' time. Sometimes, you do just have to get in the habit of looking at something almost every day to stop it getting out of control: put that back there, that over here. Otherwise, it's a bombsite.

But to help myself to do this, I've got a couple of systems that you can use, too.

Why I'm A Bulk Buyer...

Where I live there aren't that many food refill shops where you can take your own containers and cut down on all the packaging. If there were, I would get my staples there. But when Joe and I tried to drive out to different refill shops, I realised it might not be so eco-friendly for us – driving there, driving back! I also found it wasn't as economical as I thought it would be. So what I do instead is buy in bulk – the things you use all the time, that won't go off for ages. For example, you can go online (I use www.wholefoodsmarket.co.uk) and buy a five-kilo bag of oats that works out much cheaper than a box from the shop. I know that sounds like a lot, but it could be all the oats you need for the next six months.

I've got really useful plinth drawers underneath my kitchen cupboards, where I store all the stuff I buy in bulk: my bulk tea, bulk nuts, bulk everything, really! And then I just decant them into labelled jars in the pantry cupboard, as and when they are running low. Now, I know everyone doesn't have spare drawers, but your bulk bags just need to be kept in a cool, dry place – perhaps your shed, or the garage.

It will mean fewer trips to the shop. Everything's cheaper. And it all looks really organised, because you only have a jar of each item out in your cupboard, rather than scruffy bags leaking everywhere. It really does make life easier.

...AND A LABEL LOVER!

I love labels – I get pretty stick-on ones for my containers from my sister Jemma's company (www.thelabellady.shop). Obviously, they tell you what's inside, so you're not getting mixed up and pouring salt in your tea. But I think, ultimately, the advantage is the aesthetic – if you like the way your things look, it definitely motivates you to keep them tidy. For instance, if I have bought icing sugar, and I have a beautifully labelled glass jar with a nice wooden lid ready for it, I will pour it in and put that jar back neatly. If not, I'll just shove the new bag in the cupboard and could easily end up with five bags in there because I don't know what I've got. So if in doubt, label it!

♥ ♥
♥ *Tip* Don't forget your lazy Susans! I use these rotating trays in my cupboards to store things like cans. That way, you won't struggle to reach a can hidden at the back of a cupboard – just give it a twirl and grab the one you want.

WHY THIS WAY WORKS

Honestly, if you follow a few of these tips, you won't need to do massive tidies of your kitchen that often. When every cupboard has a reason for being (herbs, snacks, plates, etc.) and a system, it is quite hard for it all to get ridiculously messy. Everything's got a place and it's not that difficult to put everything back as you go. That's why, by tackling one messy cupboard at a time, I can just about stay on top of mine.

My kitchen can still feel covered in *stuff*: the kids' stuff, stuff that should be in the utility room, stuff that belongs upstairs. But if I know where it all belongs and everything has a home, it's so much less overwhelming when it comes to sorting it. In that case, I will either get up really early (earlier than usual) or leave it until the kids have gone to bed, if I'm still able to keep my eyes open. I'll just go in there and go mad, putting everything back where it should be! I will also deep clean: wipe down the cupboard fronts, give the tiles on my splashback a good scrub, and get in all the grout. Once it's all done, it almost feels like a brand new kitchen.

And that's the whole point of organising, be it a room, cupboard or drawer. Nothing's perfect all the time. However, when it's organised, most of the time it's maintainable, because you have a system and everything has got a place.

♡

Tidy Outdoors

It's at this point in the day, just before lunch, when we're getting out into the garden for some fresh air. If it's not a school day, I'll force Zach and Leighton outside.

I'm so grateful that we have outdoor space, it's just such a blessing, so I want the boys to appreciate it. Joe lived in an apartment before we moved in together, while I was in a townhouse with a tiny square patio and a bit of grass. So when we were looking for a place, a good garden was the one thing we really wanted. And we're so lucky to have it, especially with four boys between us, who are so high-energy and need somewhere to burn it all off.

♡ My Life As A Serial (Plant) Killer ♡

My mum's always had green fingers, like her dad, my granddad, who had a full vegetable patch. So I picked up some of the basics from them. But I will say, a lot of people are really intimidated by the garden, myself included. Sometimes it seems much more complicated than it is. It's a slow process, so when something doesn't happen straight away, that can be really disheartening. And I've killed quite a few plants so far. I've got to the point that when something does grow, I'm like, woohoo, it's an actual plant! I honestly feel like I've created life.

So, I have a lot of lavender bushes that pretty much look after themselves. Lavender also makes me less anxious (I'm not imagining it: they use it in aromatherapy to help that) – it's one of my favourite plants. I've some geraniums, which are colourful and easy to care for, and I've planted climbing jasmine that's reached the top of my trellis and I've now got to get it to grow out to the side. And I've got a rosebush, but nothing's happened there. At least the neighbour's roses come over my fence!

Indoors, I don't do very well with real plants. I've got cactuses, succulents – plants that do best when you leave them alone, so they're great if you don't want to maintain them – and fake plants (my fejkas!).

♥ ♥
♥ *Tip* You can fake it in your garden, too. I like to have floral decorations around my front door, to match the different seasons. And when a seasonal display isn't on the door, I'll often hang it on the trellis. So, in summer I might have a trellis covered in autumn flowers! They're so pretty, I think I might as well display them.

♥ If You're Starting From Scratch ♥

Creating a nice garden doesn't have to be a huge headache. When we moved in, the garden was so lifeless. I just got out there with my friend Penny one summer's day and we planted it all. We lined my sleepers (I've got raised flowerbeds, with a wooden 'sleeper' keeping the soil in) with about eight centimetres of soil, before we started planting. Then we covered the soil with protective black mesh liner (what's known as landscape fabric), cutting holes to dig in the plants and for them to grow through. You have to remember to leave a nice space in between the baby plants because they're only small, but they will get bigger. Cover the liner with more soil, woodchips/ decorative bark, gravel or little stones (it hides the liner and looks really pretty); I went for white stones. Although I will say one thing is an absolute nightmare: I am constantly picking out brown leaves from those bloomin' white stones! If I did it again I would go for woodchips or decorative bark – it's miles cheaper and would blend in better with any falling leaves.

♥ ♥

♥ *Tip* Don't be afraid to ask questions – everyone's got to start somewhere. I still don't know half the stuff I need to know in the garden. I'd love to know how to grow something a bit more sophisticated than lavender! And when I first moved in, I would ask the garden centre everything. Can I keep that plant alive? Is it easy? How does it do in the winter? So go to your local garden centre and ask away.

♥ My Number One ♥ Gardening Tip
(AND WHY I WANT YOU TO GIVE IT A GO!)

The one thing I would say, if you're not used to planting stuff or you're a bit apprehensive about it, is just give it time. I'm an I-want-it-yesterday type of person, so a lot of the time I'm rushing and I want an immediate payoff. That's why I love organising – the minute I've done it, it's done and I can see it. Gardening is a whole different ballgame. You have to go in there knowing that you're not going to see any results for possibly months. My whole mindset changes when I'm in the garden.

That's something that can really centre you, as you follow the process from beginning to end. You plant something, and then you've got to spend however many days caring for it, making sure it's got sunlight, water – and there's no exact rule book for a living thing. You've got to go with what the plant looks like it wants – it's a bit of guesswork, and you've got to just give it a go! But I think it's exciting, too.

Often, people will tell us to be present and make sure we're there in the moment, enjoying every single thing – which can feel hard to do. And this is one area where it's OK if you're not present. Time passes so quickly you don't even notice it going by. Life's going on, and six months later you turn around and think, what's happened to the garden? Everything's grown! I don't know what that feeling is. But I love it.

Little things I love

There's something really special about anything you achieve in the garden. I had some parsley that had turned yellow and looked like death. I told myself, I'm going to repot it and I'm going to talk to it every day and just try to rescue it... When it did recover, it really made my whole week – I felt like I'd saved a life!

Tidy
YOUR OUTDOOR SPACE

I find the garden is the hardest space in the house to keep tidy – it is my nemesis! The boys are in and out of it all day, you've got leaves blowing all over the place in the autumn, or everyone leaving their cups and glasses out there in the summer. And, of course, outside we have all the messy stuff like the sandpit and Rex's little mud kitchen, and we'll be potting plants out there, too.

The way I tackle it is, everything has a place in the garden, and I will put it back every single day: the boys' bikes, Rex's toys, the glasses people leave lying about! Then the rest Joe and I do as and when. Most of the time, we just sweep up the leaves and water the plants. If there are any dead ones, I deadhead them (which means removing the dead flower heads) with my garden clippers. My lawn is fake, so we never have to mow it. Honestly, I can't think of anything worse! The only thing I miss is the smell of cut grass. We jet wash the patio a few times through the summer, and leave it over the winter. Once winter sets in and the rain starts coming, we don't really need to water the plants either.

On top of that, every quarter Joe and I will have a proper deep clean: we will go full out! Clear all the rubbish, jet wash the patio, hoover the grass. (Yes, I take the Hoover out there and give it a good go.) But that's about it. I couldn't have it any other way, our lives are so busy. I don't have loads of special kit, either. We bought a hoe because I kept spelling Joe's name as Hoe by mistake on Instagram – but we've never used it. I recently bought a leaf sucker/blower/mulcher, whatever it's called. And it's changed my life. I must say, it's much easier than sweeping up the leaves and picking them up by hand.

Of course, you might want to swap the vacuum for a lawnmower, if you've got real grass. But once you're in the swing of things, you really don't need a complicated routine to get a garden you love. And you don't need to spend a lot of money to get it just how you want it, either.

Here are a few ideas to get you started…

♡ How To Make The ♡ Most Of A Garden

(OR, STICK UP A SHELF!)

We don't have a traditional garden shed – instead, we plastered the inside of ours, painted it and we use it as a snug for the boys. We've also set up our garage as a playroom, so they'll go in there to watch a movie or whatever. I'm all for using your space in the way that suits *you*! That means our bikes and the jet wash are kept to the side of our shed, under a cover to keep them dry. However, when I've had a traditional garage, I like to have racks fixed to the walls for the bikes, skateboards, scooters, etc, so they're not just taking up floor space.

I like to have shelves outside, too – but you don't need to spend money on expensive garden furniture. (I don't: the boys are out there kicking a football or playing basketball all day long, so it's just not worth it!) Instead, I've put up some little wooden crates as garden shelves. I just stuck some stick-on Command hooks straight onto the wood of the garden trellis, and hung the crates off those. And I'd screwed some little brass hooks into the bottom side of one crate, to hang all our garden tools up – which is a really easy way to keep them organised and accessible.

An old set of shelves also makes a great potting station. I had one that was falling apart, hammered in a few extra nails to hold it together, then gave it a lick of paint to smarten it up. Now, it's home to all the pots of herbs we're growing – and with a little mirror from Poundland fixed above it, you'd never guess I found it in the dump!

Tip If in doubt, spray paint it. I'm a mix of lazy and impatient – and spray paint's quick and dries quickly, so I use it a lot! I go for stuff that goes on pretty much any material. I mostly use Rust-Oleum, it's the best one for me.

And while we're at it, here are a few quick, easy crafting ideas to decorate your garden.

Make Up

WATERING CAN GARDEN LIGHT

A drill or screwdriver
An old watering can
A spray of fairy lights

1. Use a drill to make a few of the holes in the watering can spout/rose slightly bigger – or you could use a screwdriver and wiggle it around.

2. Then, take the spray of fairy lights (I used solar ones) and thread the strands through the holes, to be the 'water'.

3. You could leave it like that, or I looped some string around the handle of the watering can, so I could hang it at an angle off my fence post, with a nail in the fence panel to help it stay put. When it's dark, the fairy lights switch on and it looks like it's pouring light!

Make the holes bigger

Done ✓

Thread the lights through

Make Up

CHOPPING BOARD BIRDBATH

You can end up with quite a lot of empty jars or candle holders, so this is a nice thing to do with them.

A wooden chopping board or another flat piece of wood
A drill
Superglue
Four old candle holders or jars (I used brown glass ones)
Twine
Birdseed
A little fejka, if you've got one!

1. I took an old wooden chopping board – but you could use any other flat piece of wood about that size.

2. I drilled an extra hole at one end of the board (mine already had a little hole at the other) to help me hang it up later.

3. Then I superglued four empty glass candle holders to the board, so they looked like they were standing up against it.

4. Using the two holes in the board, I used loops of twine to hang it from nails in the fence. Put some birdseed in one candle holder (I filled two!), water in one for the birdbath and a fake plant in another... and the birds will come!

♥ ♥

♥ *Tip* Just soak candle holders or jars overnight in water to get the labels off. If there's any wax in there, you can pour in boiling water, leave it for a bit, and it will just rise to the top so you can lift it off when cooler. But be careful: glass containers sold with a candle should normally be heatproof, but boiling water can cause some glass to shatter. Don't just try this technique on anything glass you've got!

And if you're thinking, er, Stace, do you realise how small my garden/balcony/bit of patio is?! No, don't worry – I've been there! And a balcony can be an outdoor sanctuary, too. And I've got some suggestions for you:

Make sure to use all your *vertical* space – any walls or fences you can access. If you've got a trellis, or are able to put one up, you could attach some hooks to that and hang things straight off it.

Maybe you only have a window box or some space by your front door. There are still things you can do. When Joe had a flat with a balcony, he had a couple of nice, easy-to-care-for green plants – but a hanging basket of fuchsias would be really good, as well. And you can still grow vegetables or fruit: tomatoes, strawberries, anything like that. If I had a balcony, I'd choose geraniums – easy to look after, happy and colourful!

Outdoor storage boxes really are great if you've not got much space. You can get pretty ones in white, black and grey that come in handy for all your bits and pieces.

Which reminds me – I can't leave the garden without having a look in my junk trunk…

♡ *Put Some Junk* ♡
In Your Trunk

Remember my junk trunk? Mine's just a cheap, watertight plastic box that I keep outside. But honestly, it gives me so much joy!

It's full of old tin cans, empty candle holders and old glass jars – anything that I think I can use to make something goes into the junk trunk, and I really recommend having one. Then, if you ever think, oh, it's a shame to throw that away, that's when you put something in the junk trunk, even though someone else might call it rubbish!

Later, when you see something that inspires you, say, on Pinterest, you'll remember, ooh, I've got that old glass jar in the junk trunk, *that's* what I can make out of it. You might not necessarily know at the time what you're saving it for – it might come to you days, weeks, months afterwards! But eventually, you'll get a better sense of what you will and won't use and it will start to be obvious what to keep and what to throw away. Just make sure to wash whatever you put in there before you leave it for months… you can imagine why!

And that's it! We've sorted out the garden. So it's got to be time for a treat.

Watermelon slices

Grapes

Strawberries

Carrot peel tail

Done ✔

Snack Time

WATERMELON PIG

I make fruit animals almost every day. In summer, I make lots of watermelon ones – and a really easy one is this watermelon pig.

Watermelon
A seedless grape
A couple of strawberries
A carrot (for its peel)

1. Just cut two round slices of watermelon – one a little bit bigger than the other – and stack them on top of each other on a plate (the bigger one underneath for the body, the smaller one is the head, as if you're looking at your pig head on).

2. Cut a grape in half and add those for its eyes. Cut the top off one strawberry to make the round nose, then cut both strawberries in half to make the ears and trotters. Finish with a carrot peel tail. Oink!

♡ Hero Task ♡

HAVE A BREAK!

Surprise! I'm not about to start you on another massive tidying task here. As we've reached halfway through my day – and this book – I want you to grab a cuppa and take a moment to unwind with a bit of grown-up colouring-in. Honestly, it's so satisfying – some of my favourite things are hidden in the picture below…

Clues:

1. My (veggie-themed) pet name for the kids

2. I'm gasping for a…

3. My go-to sweet treat

4. My favourite print (Susan doesn't like it!)

5. I call him Norm

6. The prettiest pumpkin ever

Answers

1. Pickles. Did you find it? It's a picture of a real pickle, if you haven't – not Rex!

2. A lovely cup of tea

3. Daim bar – I absolutely love 'em!

4. You know that lovely leafy print you see everywhere? I've got it on some of my bedding – and every time I show it on my Insta, the same woman will message me to say it's the worst print ever, who would have that on their bed? Her name's Susan. It really cracks me up, that this one Susan constantly moans about our bedding, so now I call it the 'Susan' print, after her!

5. Norm the gnome… I made him out of Joe's old socks.

6. My beautiful unicorn pumpkin! I'll show you how to make one for Halloween, and your own gnome, later on in the book.

Easy Afternoons

And with that, it's time for some lunch! Which, in my house, is generally last night's dinner. I find lunch one of the hardest meals to cook from scratch, if I'm completely honest with you.

I'm good at breakfast – I can get up early enough to make a breakfast! And I'm pretty good around dinner, and so's Joe. But lunchtime rolls around just when you've caught up with your work, you've tidied, and you've done everything else you've got to do. You think, thank G-d I've got those leftovers in the fridge, because I can't think of anything worse than cooking a meal right now!

♡ No More 'What's For Lunch?' ♡

So, if opportunity presents itself, I *might* make something (a really easy lunch when the boys are home is my all-day breakfast bake I've already shown you) – but nine times out of ten, lunch will be leftover Bolognese, or leftover shepherd's pie. I simply make an extra portion or two whenever I cook – since we're normally two adults, two children and a baby, I'll make a meal that serves five or six and it takes a lot of pressure off. Especially as we're always being told, don't eat too much processed food, don't eat this, don't eat that. I find it all quite anxiety-inducing, what we're supposed to eat and what we're not supposed to eat. This way makes me feel like I'm eating good food every day and I don't have to do any extra cooking.

All you need to do is put one leftover portion in the fridge the night before you need it, then just heat it up for lunch the next day (if it's going to be longer than overnight, I'll stick it in the freezer). And you don't need to be cooking for a big family to do this. In fact, a lot of the time when you're living on your own, it's easy to cook too much – most recipes aren't for one, so you can end up with a meal for five! When you do that, think – brilliant, I can freeze all this.

♥ ♥
♥ Tip You might not fancy the same thing again for lunch the next day, so just get a day ahead of yourself. In our house, we might make dinner on Monday, freeze the leftovers, and have sandwiches for lunch on Tuesday – then we can save some of that dinner that we've frozen for Wednesday's lunch. Then you just stay in that pattern of being a couple of days ahead of yourself, so you don't get too bored.

If all the kids are home with me – say, if it's a school holiday – I will make a week's worth of sandwiches in different flavours and put them in the freezer at the start of the week. Then, every night, I just leave some sandwiches in the fridge to thaw, ready for the next day. I will do bagels with ham and cheese, cream cheese and cucumber sandwiches, jam, peanut butter – there's not much that can't freeze (although Marmite doesn't come out that great, I don't think). It means the boys' lunches are sorted for the whole week – because it's hectic when they are home, I don't care what anyone says. Of course, it's lovely – you think, oh, I'll get to spend all that time with them. But literally two days in and you're pulling your hair out! So make it easy on yourself.

Meal Time

SHAPE UP YOUR SANDWICHES

To make it fun, just use ordinary cookie cutters to press out the middle of each sandwich. Don't throw away the rest – I will serve my boys a whale/dinosaur/seahorse and give them the outline, too! That way you don't waste anything and they'll still enjoy it.

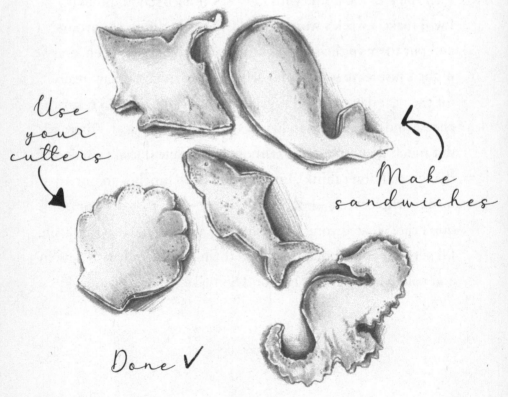

Use your cutters

Make sandwiches

Done ✔

Snack Time

CHOCOLATE APPLES

For a sweet treat, I love the idea of chocolate apples. But these are much easier to eat than a whole apple on a stick (and you get a bit more chocolate to enjoy, too).

An apple or two
Extra-long cocktail sticks
Bar of milk chocolate, melted in a bowl (either in the
*   microwave or over a pan of simmering water)*

1. Slice an apple from the top down, so you get nice slim slices that are in that apple-y shape (of course, they'll be smaller when you're slicing near the edges – that's OK). I don't throw away the core – the pips will fall out anyway, and it tastes the same as the rest of the apple to me!

2. Then, stick an extra-long cocktail stick through the middle of each slice, dip it in melted chocolate and leave to cool and set on a wire rack (so it's easier to peel off). They taste delicious and they look cute as well.

Apple slice →

Dipped in chocolate ↗

Done ✔

After lunch, I'll do a quick clear up. Joe would load the dishwasher three times a day if it was up to him, whereas I do it as I go along, washing up little bits and pieces. My mum never had a dishwasher or a microwave, so I just never used them. And I might give the surfaces a very quick tidy and wipe, grabbing the stuff from under the sink.

Tidy
UNDER THE SINK

In my kitchen, under the sink is for my everyday cleaning stuff: a surface spray, dishwasher tablets, washing-up liquid, a glass or window cleaner. I like to keep them in a white IKEA box (with a 'cleaning' label on it) that I arrange by the biggest product down to the smallest. If I put the big bottles at the back, then the next level is the stuff that's not so tall, and so on, I can see everything in there. All my cleaning cloths go under the sink as well, clipped to a tension rod the same way I have my crisps – I hang them up at the back, in colour order. I also hang up washing-up brushes – and anything else I can, really! You can usually tie string through the hole in the bottom of something like a washing-up brush and clip that up as well.

It is one of those corners of the home that can get messy, because you're constantly using the stuff in there – and not everyone puts it back properly, and sometimes you just chuck it back in there yourself! But it's a really nice, easy place to tidy the way I have set it up, because it's just a box of cleaning stuff and a lot of cloths. Because there's a system it is so simple: just put it all back where it belongs and it looks tidy again.

HOW TO ORGANISE ANYTHING

By this point, you may be wondering, hold on – you're organising by size and colour here. So do I do mine by size? Colour? And what about grouping products of the same brands together? (Which I also like to do sometimes.) Really, like I've said before, the main thing is that you can *see* what you've got. For me, this helps me stop overbuying – if I leave it all in a big messy pile, I will just keep buying… and buying… and buying… every time I go to Tesco. All of a sudden, I've got twenty-two scourers! We end up buying so much more than what we need a lot of the time. And with some things it's OK because they're not perishable, it's just a bit annoying. But with other things that may go off, you've just wasted money, which I hate. After that, it's a matter of personal preference as to how you organise. Some people prefer things in size order, others go by colour, and some people prefer things in brand order (so that everything from the same brand is grouped together).

My personal preference is generally to go by size first. I really like colour order – it makes me happy. But when I put things in colour order, if they're not in size order, too – if everything I'm lining up by colour is a totally different size, say – that annoys me. There's something about the unevenness of it all that really gets on my nerves. So I'll go in size order first, and try to balance out the colours as best I can. Just remember, it's up to you to pick a system that suits whatever you're tidying – so there's no way you can get it wrong!

WHY BEING TIDY WILL SAVE YOU MONEY!

When I was younger, we didn't have money to buy much – it was like, you get one cleaning cloth and that's it! So I've carried that with me. I know, deep down, I don't need a hundred of everything, it's just not necessary. And so I try really hard to not overbuy things. But I can still end up buying more than I need, and that makes me feel a bit sick. If I feel like I've bought things because I thought I didn't have it, then realise I've got loads of them already, I think, what a waste – I could have saved that money for something else. So, being tidy and organised can save you money. And who doesn't want that?

♥ ♥
♥ *Tip* I don't have bins under the sink, or a standalone bin – mine is built into a pullout drawer in the kitchen. I'd always recommend that, if you ever get the option. When I've had a freestanding bin, Pickle starts getting into it, and the older kids chuck stuff around it. Sometimes they seem to be totally unable to find the inside of the bin, and I think, what the hell is wrong with you – there's a banana on top of the lid! But when your bin is built into a drawer, everyone has to physically open it to put their rubbish in, they can't leave things on top, and it can't get knocked over. And I do find that a little bit easier.

♥ Time To Tidy ♥

After lunch, I tend not to do as much tidying as in the morning. If I do it in the afternoon, I feel I tidy, and before I know it the kids come home, ransack it and then it's bed! So, often I will tackle a tidying job first thing in the morning so I can actually get some enjoyment out of it, or last thing at night once the kids have gone to bed, so I can wake up to it. Of course, you need to find the times that suit you to tidy – which may be totally different! It's whatever works for you. But the great thing about having that pattern in my life is that, if I'm not working, it frees up a bit of the afternoon for me.

Little things I love:
Me time and crafting

When I'm at home, if the opportunity presents itself – the big boys are at school, and Rex is having a nap – I will get my glue gun out. This is gold dust. Those moments when you get the chance to just sit and do something you love, whether it be exercise, cooking, eating, singing or dancing, just to have those moments is bliss. So I grab them by both hands whenever I can.

If the boys are home, then I try to encourage them to enjoy my favourite hobbies with me, and I'm so glad they like making stuff because to have that bit of common ground can be lifesaving.

Make Up

LAVA LAMP

This is so easy and really fun. Kids actually love it.

A clear glass bottle
Baby oil. You can use any oil, but I like this because it's so
see-through
Food colouring
An effervescent (fizzy) tablet – we use the Milton sterilising
tablets I use for Rex's baby bottles

1. Take a glass bottle – I used one of my bathroom empties.
    (If you need to get the label off, an easy way is to just fill the
    bottle carefully with boiling water, if it's heatproof. After a
    while, the heat melts the glue and you should be able to peel
    the label away – see also page 106.)

2. Pour in enough water, so it's a bit over halfway full, then top
    up with oil, a dash of food colouring and then the tablet,
    broken up. I used a funnel so it didn't spill, but don't worry if
    you don't have one.

3. Then, the ingredients start to react together – that's when the
    'lava' effect begins. It doesn't go on forever and ever, but you
    get a good few days of it.

Make Up

PLAY SAND

For this, all you need is some scoops of breakfast cereal and a food processor. Blend the cereal until it's like a powder. Then chuck it in a little tray. I give it to Rex to play with. He can even eat it if he wants – but he just loves the feel of it. Sometimes, I'll blend a few different types of cereal separately – Rice Krispies, Frosties and Cheerios, say – and put them in a tray or baby dish with little sections, so he can feel the different types of 'sand'. And I'll watch him notice the difference – it's really interesting for me, too!

P.S. This is another good one for a baby on a rainy day: I got some tissue paper in different colours, screwed up pieces into little balls, then put them all in a colander for Rex. He picked every single ball out through the holes (and I just kept putting them all back in). Silly little things like that, they love! It kept him busy for ages.

And, of course, if I really love what I've just made, I'll show it to you, too!

♡ Good To Share ♡

As you probably know, once I've made something or tidied a corner or maybe been for a walk in the woods, I'll often share it on Instagram. After all, if I've got time to clean a cupboard, I've got time to record it! And I've always been like this: even before Instagram existed, whenever we went on a walk or a trip, I would have still videoed it, taken pictures, collected souvenirs. Because I just love making memories – I love sitting with my boys watching home videos and remembering places we've been and things we've done together. So I would do all that anyway! I am just doing the same thing these days – but now I'll make a little montage and upload it.

And I like sharing what I do with other people, because it's like meeting your friends and chatting about your day or painting a wall you're proud of and showing your family.

You just feel like you are not alone – and knowing there are other people out there who find the same things satisfying and enjoyable makes you feel confident enough to share more.

Even if I make something that turns out a bit rubbish, I just love the messages when people say, 'You made it – so who cares what it looks like so long as you enjoyed it? Keep going!' It makes you feel like nothing you do is ever going to be rubbish, really – that even if it doesn't come out how you want it, it's still *you* and everything that you stand for. Which is how I want you to feel about whatever you try, too.

♡ No More Guilty Pleasures ♡

I think a lot of us – but especially parents – can feel guilty and selfish if we do something for ourselves. Sometimes, of an evening, the kids will be playing or arguing or whatever, while I'll just sit there colouring-in or sewing! And I'll think, oh G-d, I should really be splitting up this argument, or encouraging them to read the Kindle with me, or *something*. But actually, I'm a better mum if I do something that makes me happy. I can't physically be Mum twenty-four hours a day. I love being a mum and I'm grateful to be a mum, but I don't think it defines me. I am still Stacey and have to make sure that I recognise myself as Stacey, and not just 'Mum'. Otherwise, I'm just there to serve everybody else and not to make myself happy – and I don't think that benefits any of us.

Little things I love: **Colouring-in!**

I'll draw in my notepad, I'll draw my brain junk bins ready for the next few days (more on those in a bit) or my jar and I've got paint-by-numbers kits that I use, too. I won't get the paints out (because that is a bit of a faff), but I'll use my coloured pencils or gel pens.

INSTA FAMILY

Being able to be open on my Instagram and talk about the way that I'm feeling, whether good or bad, is really helpful. And quite frankly, a relief, as I couldn't be anything else. I remember when I first had Rex, I felt really down for a while. I struggled with breastfeeding and I was quite open about it on my Instagram. And the amount of people that were like, 'Oh my G-d, I went through exactly the same thing – have you tried this, have you spoken to this person or that person?' Because of speaking out, I ended up finding Rex a tongue tie specialist, who confirmed that he *was* tongue tied – which explained why it might be harder for him to breastfeed.

With things like that, Instagram is just phenomenal. You can really feel that you've got friends on there, people who have your back and will look out for you. So if you are feeling a bit unsure about sharing what you love, whether that's tidying or crafting or whatever else, have a go. You might be really surprised – in a good way! – by the reaction.

If you don't know where to start with doing something for yourself, you could just think about setting aside a crafty drawer – and start adding bits and pieces, so that it's quicker and easier to make something when you *do* get the chance. My crafty drawers are in the cupboard under the stairs. I need to stay on top of my crafts, otherwise I'll never find anything and I can't do the things I love, so I've been quite vigilant about that. In fact, I've recently bought myself a crafts trolley, so I've got even more space for my supplies! Which means when the urge to have a big tidying and crafting session hits, I know where to start…

♡ Hero Task ♡
SORT YOUR UTILITY ROOM

With my utility room, I really was starting from scratch: nothing had a place or a home. It was dark and dingy and black and grey in there, and it was bugging me so much. It sounds silly, but I didn't want to do any of my washing because I just didn't want to be in there. I thought, I'm going to find the cheapest, most effective way of transforming this room because

I'm getting behind with my laundry! But I didn't want to pay for brand new cupboards, because there was nothing wrong with them. And it's hard to part with your money on something that really isn't in disrepair.

So instead I did a bit of research and found out that you can change the whole colour of your kitchen or utility room with vinyl – a roll of self-adhesive film (basically, sticky-backed plastic!) that covers your cupboard doors, drawers and worktops. It changed the room from dark and dingy to pink and white, which I absolutely love.

♥ ♥

Tip You can find rolls of sticky vinyl online for about six pounds each (look for 'vinyl sticker'). The best thing to do is measure the surfaces you want to cover to make sure you're ordering the right amount. My utility room took me two rolls – one white, one pink – to cover two cupboard doors, three drawers and a work surface about two metres by one metre.

There are lots of detailed YouTube tutorials, but basically it's a bit like adding sticky-backed plastic to your school books (if you had to do that, too)! Measure it as best you can to fit your surfaces, but always go over a little bit because you don't want to be short. Then I found that if I sprayed a tiny bit of water under each section as I applied the vinyl, it made it easier to rearrange it if a bubble appeared. If there were any bubbles left over, I actually got the hairdryer, and with the heat and the force of the air from that, some of them disappeared. With the worst ones, I got a tiny needle and let the air out. Then I used a Stanley knife to trim around the vinyl edges.

Lastly, I just had to finish it off with mastic – that clear sealing stuff that stops water getting between the countertop and the sink. It comes in a tube with an attachment, and you just push it out and use your finger to flatten it out. I've only added clear mastic around the sink, and not the edges of the worktop, so it's easy to remove... in case the next person who lives here doesn't want a bright pink utility!

♥ ♥

Tip With DIY jobs, a lot of the time, I'm just typing exactly what's in my head into Google: 'How do I mastic the sink at home?' And then it will come up with different videos, images, articles. I'm such a visual learner, so I always watch the videos to see exactly what they're doing step by step, but you'll find what suits you best.

SETTING UP SYSTEMS

Next, I thought OK, now I need systems in here. I need everything in here to have a place that works for me. That's really important.

At the time, one cupboard in the utility room was the shoe cupboard. It didn't make sense for our shoes to be in there – every time the boys needed to put theirs on or take them off they'd have to go in there, and all the mud would go everywhere. Now, we keep our shoes under the stairs in the hallway, which makes more sense – as that's where we take our shoes off, as we come in. Everyone's allowed maximum of two pairs of shoes downstairs: a nice pair and a casual pair. And if you don't want to wear those, you can swap 'em for a pair in your room. That system is effective – the boys can't be bothered to go upstairs so they just wear those two pairs each, which is perfect!

THE POWER OF PINK

Next, I filled that empty cupboard with cleaning products. I keep the stuff I use every day under the sink in the kitchen, so this was my extras – spare sponges, cloths and multipurpose sprays – as well as colour catchers, stain removers, heavy floor cleaner – the things I don't use all the time. I decided that because the room was pink I'd start buying cleaning products that came in pink packaging, where possible, and store them in pink baskets to match (I bought mine from Dunelm). Now, that cupboard is a dream. Instead of having my cleaning products shoved under the sink in that room, just seeing them looking all shiny and pink and pretty makes me think, I actually want to use them – I *want* to clean!

♥ ♥

♥ *Tip* As much as I love my pink products, I also try really hard to make sure everything in my house is not full of harmful chemicals. Brands like Bio-D, Ecover and Method also sell in bulk, which cuts down on packaging and works out cheaper, too. So, I buy fabric softener and washing liquid in big five- to ten-litre bottles that I decant into glass bottles from IKEA, and I buy my washing-up liquid in a big packet that I keep in the utility, too. And if you're wondering what happens to all the cleaning products that I don't need to see in that room? They're under the utility sink!

Then I got crafting. Because the room was so bright and open, I knew exactly what would go in there. I ordered strips of fake flowers to line the backs of my shelves (using stick-on decorating clips from Command to hold them up). And I put pink pampas grass into an old perfume bottle I use as a vase. That made me really happy.

Make Up

FRESH (LOOKING) FLOWER FRAMES

Clear glass photo frames
Fake flowers

TK Maxx is one of my favourite shops, but also one of my least favourite: you can go in there wanting something, but it's so random as to what they'll actually have! So I try not to head there with anything in my mind. It was there that I found the three frames that are now on the wall in my utility room. They're just two sheets of glass held in a wire frame, and I stuck real flowers in between them. I thought, it's so simple and so cheap, and it looks amazing. And then the flowers died...

I knew they would, of course, but I was hoping to make dried flowers! However, picture frames are not airtight, and because there's nothing to soak up the moisture, the flowers rotted instead. If you do want to dry flowers, put them between parchment paper, press that in a book or under a doormat for a few weeks and they'll dry out really nicely. In this case, I really wanted bright colours, not soft and faded. So I decided to put fake flowers in there instead, and they'll always be vibrant.

Happy Hometime

After lunch and a bit of playtime with Rex, soon it's time for us to walk round and pick up Leighton from school. Zach is the last one back, usually about four o'clock, and then all my boys are home again, which I love.

And one thing I find that helps when you all get in is having a place for everything – even if people don't always stick to it!

First, you've got to have somewhere to put your keys, so you're never running round thinking, where the hell are they? If you've got a nice side table, then a lovely bowl would do – if you've a candle that's run out, but you still love the look of the holder it came in, just boil some water to pour in it, to lift out any excess wax (see page 106), and then use that to chuck your keys in. (Of course, I would put a label on it that says 'keys'!) Or, you could use an old chopping board, screw in some gold hooks for your keys and hang that on the wall. You could even just have a hook! Depending on what type of wall you're drilling into, all you need is a suitable rawlplug and a screw-in hook and it can be as simple as that.

♡ A Quick Drilling Lesson ♡

You don't ever just drill a screw into a wall – you do always have to use a rawlplug, which is a little plastic holder for the screw. It depends on what kind of wall you've got as to what type of rawlplug you use. Then, you get your drill bit – the piece you put in the drill to actually make the hole in the wall – which will be specific to what you're drilling into. So, if you're drilling into tile, you get a tile drill bit; if you're drilling into brick, you get a brick drill bit. You can Google them to see exactly what they are.

Before you start drilling anything, check for pipes and electrics. Make sure you have a pipe and electric tester for this, they are cheap to buy and easy to use… no one wants to burst a pipe to hang up a set of keys. Once you've checked it's safe to drill, the best thing you can do is measure the screw you're using against the end of your drill bit, then put a bit of tape on the drill bit at the point where the screw finishes. That will mean when you drill, you just drill up to that bit of tape and it stops you going deeper than you need. Then hammer your rawlplug into the hole you've made, and you're ready to go! You could use your drill to insert the screw – just put the right head on your drill – or you could use a normal screwdriver, at that point.

♥ ♥
♥ *Tip* In every good toolkit there should be a pipe and wire tester, to make sure there's no water pipes or electricity wires in the wall where you're about to drill. If you run that over the area you're looking at, you should be safe to go ahead.

But here's what we made to sort our keys out (turn over the page).

Make Up

HOUSEKEY HOLDER

Lego figurines
Lego pieces
A pot

Leighton and I went through the boys' Lego and found a little
man who looked a bit like Joe and a little woman who looked
a bit like me. Then we glued a thin piece of Lego – a flat white
rectangle – to the outside of a little glass pot I had. We attached
the little Lego figurines to the rectangle (they just clip on – that's
the beauty of Lego), so they were stuck to the outside of the pot.
Then I drilled a little hole in each of two smaller pieces of Lego
and threaded the ring of my keys onto one piece, and Joe's keys
onto the other. Now, all our miscellaneous keys – window and
shed keys and all of that stuff – go into the pot itself, which we
keep on the edge of a shelf. And then my keys clip under the
Lego 'Stacey', and the other set clip under the Lego 'Joe'.

While we were homeschooling in lockdown, we found it really difficult to remember where everything the boys used for school was. They had one big folder each for everything, but then they'd get everything in it out to find the one thing they needed, and somehow lose stuff. So we were forced to find a system that worked. First, I bought a set of drawers to make the boys a homework and schoolwork cabinet. I labelled one side for Leighton and one side for Zach. Now, we have carried on this system, and as soon as they get back from school, they empty their bags into their drawers and work out what they need out to do their homework. And then before they go to bed, they go into their drawers and get everything out that they need to have with them for school the next day and put it in their bag.

Of course, kids won't *always* stick to a system. It's funny, because I've got drawers under my stairs for all the shoes – but the kids still just open the cupboard and kick their shoes straight in! So it's maybe not surprising that the cupboard under the stairs is the messiest part of my house by a mile…

UNDER THE STAIRS

In our house, this is the one space that's always a bloomin' mess. Inside, it's a mix of things that don't go anywhere else. There's the mop bucket – it's giant, and where else do you keep a mop bucket? There are backpacks lined up on the floor. Then on one wall are all the mops and brooms; the back is for electrics and the fuse box, so we can't hang anything there. To the left are the drawers where we keep the shoes. And the back of the door is where my Hoover hangs, with all the attachments for that. So it's not that I haven't tried to sort it out! And one thing that does really help is the peg board, with little elastic hooks to keep things like the broom off the floor.

Peg It Up

Peg boards can be really handy: these are simply big boards with lots of little holes in them that you can fix to the wall to create extra storage space. You can get them from a pound shop, but IKEA's come with all sorts of different clever attachments, so that's what I've got under the stairs. There are little jars and trays you can easily fix on; hooks to hangs things up; elastic cords where you put one end into the pegboard, loop the cord under your broom head and hook the other side around it to keep it in place. I've drilled my peg board to the wall: I put some rawlplugs into the wall, then added screws through the peg board to keep it up – because the board's got little holes in it anyway, you don't need to drill any more. (Just make sure you pick a screw with a fatter head than the hole.) And don't screw the board absolutely flat onto the wall – leave it about a centimetre away, so you can still make use of the peg board's holes to hook things into them.

That helps me keep everything off the floor – or that's the idea. Because that cupboard is just the place where we shove everything in. If we get a lot of deliveries, the empty boxes end up going in there before we recycle them. All the shopping bags are kept in there, too, but then when we come back from the shops, people (sometimes that includes me) just throw them back in there. So then people see that mess and take advantage of it – 'oh, it's the messy cupboard, I'm just going to chuck things in.' If we go away, I guarantee you that afterwards, instead of emptying his suitcase, Joe will put his bag in the cupboard under the stairs – and a week later I'll discover where all the dirty washing from holiday went! It's just that kind of cupboard. Sometimes I'll open it and can't even close it again. That's when I know I need to attack it!

Really, it's just one of those things that you have to live with being a little bit messy. Not every cupboard can be perfectly organised. You do have to have somewhere where all of the random stuff can go until you find a minute to sort it out. And that is what that cupboard is for us! Sometimes you just have to close the door on a cupboard (if you can!). Sometimes it's OK to look at something and say, that is where all my random bits and pieces are.

Snack Time

AFTER-SCHOOL SPECIAL

After school, I will always give the boys a snack. If I didn't, they would just eat the entire contents of the fridge. Sometimes I have to give them a sandwich before dinner because they are so hungry!

But my kids are not actually massive junk eaters. I think because I don't hide the snacks away and they can go in that cupboard whenever they want, they actually get bored of them, and would rather I make them something. I have tried the opposite approach: for years, I wouldn't give them juice (because it makes them really hyper), so when they finally did get juice, I wished I'd never made it such a big deal. For a while, it was like junkies with crack! Now that they know they can have it, they actually prefer water.

Here are a few of my favourite snacks to make...

Oreo spiders: Just shove pieces of Matchmaker chocolate sticks in each side of an Oreo cookie, to make a cute spider with legs (snap the sticks into shorter bits so they're not too long). You can add two icing googly 'eyes' that you can find in the supermarket – stick them in place with blobs of white icing.

142

Creamy cow: Cut a cream cheese sandwich into two oval shapes, to make your cow's head and body (the easiest way to do this is with a pair of scissors). Arrange pieces of the crust around them for ears, legs and a tail, then add a bigger piece of crust for the nose. Place a few blackberries in random places, for its patches. You could finish it with a couple of blueberries for its nostrils.

Olive penguin: Your penguin is going to stand on a slice of carrot for its 'feet'. Add a small ball of cheese – mozzarella works – for the body. Cut an olive in half for the arms, top with another olive for the head, and stick a little piece of carrot into that for a beak!

Banana bread dinosaur: Cut a slice from a loaf of banana bread (from the shops is fine) for the dinosaur's body. Then, cut a banana in half down the middle. Arrange one half at a corner of the banana bread to be the dinosaur's head and neck, cut two little bits off the rest of the banana to make feet, and use the last piece for the tail.

Tip It's impossible to keep everything organised and perfect all the time. And if there's a place where you want to let it all go, that's fine – be proud of it! Enjoy your naughty cupboard.

♡ Walking It Off ♡

I find the more that I walk the kids, the better they go to bed!
They are so full of energy, they just need it run out of them. Joe's
really good – he's my saving grace when it comes to tiring the
boys out, because he will play-fight with them, chase them, and
I just think, thank G-d for that! I've been so lucky that they'll go
to him. But even if he's not around, I'll just have to get them out,
run about, take them to the swings or on their bikes – anything
to get 'em exhausted! So when they get back they can do their
homework, have their dinner, have a little play, and then go
to bed. Sometimes the older boys won't go for a walk – they'll
turn into Kevin and Perry. And sometimes I can't be bothered
to argue, so I'll let them fester. But I do really try to get them
outside – even if it's raining. Anything to make bedtime easier.

Little things I love:
Rainy walks in the woods

My kids love nothing more than wellies, a raincoat and a walk in
the rain, and so do I now – rainy walks can be lovely.

Make Up

EMPTY BOTTLE PENCIL CASES

The kids thought these were hilarious.

Old plastic bottles, rinsed clean
Zips (one per bottle; I used a red one to match the ketchup
bottle I'd picked)

1. First, stand a bottle upright on its base, then cut the top off the bottle at its 'shoulders', so a bit up from the middle.

2. Then, glue one side of the zip around the open edge of the bottle's base and trim it to fit (cutting from the end of the zip without the little metal base, of course). Don't cut it so it is exactly the same length as the edge of the bottle – leave a little flap.

3. Next, unzip the zip to make it easier to glue the other side of the zip piece around the edge of the other bottle half. When you zip it up again, you've got a pencil case!

Cut off top

Glue on zip

Done ✔

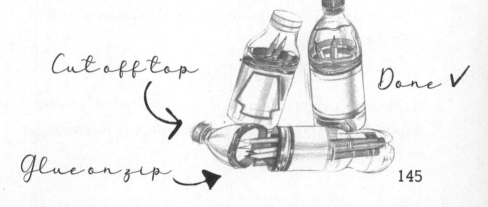

♥ ♥
♥ *Tip* I crafted some stationery organisers for me out of empty old tin cans. Just wrap them in whatever you want (once they are clean), gluing it into place: I did one in the rustic string I like to use; another in a piece of an old jumper.

After homework, the kids can play. The older boys are not really into toys anymore – they might do a bit of Lego, or they'll get their Nerf guns out maybe and have a little Nerf war with Joe – but most of the games they play will be Minecraft or something like that, so they're not that messy! They are allowed to play computer games after school, but not every day – we've got a one day on, one day off system here.

♥ ♥
♥ *Tip* The cupboard underneath the telly is for the boys' consoles and computer games. To keep them tidy, I've got a piece of peg board in there – just propped against the back of the cupboard, with attachments (shelves, jars for the power leads and wire brackets to hold the consoles) to keep all their kit organised.

Mostly the activities that my kids will do (outside of playing their PlayStations) will be the stuff they do with me: baking and

146

crafting. But Pickle's messy! His stuff will be all over the place. Sometimes I'll clear it up myself, if it's a case of just getting it into the toy box. But I do try to teach Rex to help – I'll say, 'Come on now, tidy up time.' And I'm sure now, even though he's only eighteen months old, he tells me to tidy up. Even at his age, I'm sure he understands what I'm saying. I've found that actually, the younger they are, the more they enjoy copying what I do. So if I tidy up, he tidies up. I'm enjoying this while I can, as when they get older, they clock on to it and being lazy is a lot easier.

THE KIDS' ROOMS

The older boys have to look after their own rooms. I will change their sheets over when they need it, but outside of that, I wash my hands of them. I just feel like if I do everything for them, they'll never be able to look after themselves. I really want to make a point that they know how to use the washing machine, they know how to wash up, cook and how to look after themselves. It doesn't always mean they do it, because they don't, but I know that they can – so if push comes to shove and they need to do it, then they will. They're the kind of kids that will live in filth in their bedrooms until they can't take it anymore. And then they will tidy it!

147

♡ *Hero Task* ♡
SORT YOUR WIRE DRAWER

Which is a bit like how I was with my wire drawer. It took me ages – hours and hours – to sort it out, but I was so pleased when I did. Everyone's got that wire drawer, or wire cupboard, where you keep all your electrical stuff – chargers, leads, computer bits and TV cables – and it can easily get to be a bit of a tip. But don't panic: just start as we always do, and take every single wire out of that drawer!

Then the main thing you need to tackle, once you've got it all out and have had a look through, is sorting through the wires into piles: what you actually use and want to keep; what you don't use and are going to get rid of (and, if there's any you need but haven't got, make a note so you can pick some up later). Anything you are not sure about, you can stick in a Maybe pile – but it should be fairly easy to know if it's for the Keep pile or not, once you've worked out if you still use it.

What you'll probably find is that you have so many wires for things that you don't even own anymore. When I did my wire drawer, I found chargers for an iPhone 1, my first ever iPhone – I haven't seen an iPhone 1 for about fifteen years and I can't imagine anyone coming round and asking for an iPhone 1 charger! So why did I still have one? And there were SCART leads in there, cables which link your TV to your devices – which I didn't need, because my telly was already set up and working. But we end up holding on to these unnecessary wires just because they came in the packet with something, and we worry we might need them one day. Most of the time, you don't! You can get rid of them responsibly – check with your local authority or a campaign called www.recycleyourelectricals.org. uk to see the options near you.

I've a few exceptions to that: apart from the wires I know I use regularly, I might keep some HDMIs – these are the wires you plug into your TV to connect to a DVD player or PlayStation or an Xbox or something else like that – as I find they can come in handy. And I would also keep hold of spare chargers for your devices (because people are always losing their phone chargers, in particular) and any laptop leads.

But if you look at a wire and think, I've got no idea what that's for, so I'd better keep it, I still say, it's time to get rid of it. If everything in your house is working, you're probably never going to find out what it's for! And if you do happen to come across something that you suddenly need a wire for, it's so easy these days to search for that wire online and have it arrive in the post in a day or two.

ROUTING MY WIRES

Before I arranged all the wires I was keeping in the drawer, I bought little sticky-backed wire organisers to place in the bottom first. Basically, each one is a bit of rubber: you put the wire into a gap in the middle and it closes itself around it. And what I did was roll up every single wire (around its plug, if it had one) leaving a tiny bit sticking out at the end to clip into one of these little wire organisers. Now, when I open the drawer, I can see every single wire that I've got – and not only that, but I can see the little attachment on the end of it straight away. That means when someone asks, have we got a charger for this or that, I can instantly see if we've got something that fits it, rather than scrabbling around for ages.

Some people might say, oh my G-d, who's got the time to sit there doing that? But if you think of the amount of time you can spend looking for the right wire in the wire drawer every day, it balances itself out. After all, most of us have lost more than a few minutes tracking down some wire for the PlayStation that's gone missing!

GET A BATTERY PACK

There are some things that I wouldn't put in my wire drawer, however, like my batteries. I used to keep my spare batteries loose, in little drawers. And then one day someone said to me, 'I don't think you can keep open batteries touching each other...' I found out that if the positive and negative ends/sides touch each other, it can make them short-circuit and leak, which in rare cases can cause fires. So, I bought a battery organiser from Amazon that looks like a little suitcase with different-sized slots inside, to keep them all separate.

Honestly, I get so much joy out of organising my batteries. There are so many times, especially at Christmas and birthdays, when I'm looking for a certain type of battery, and I'll see instantly if we've got one. I never have to root around the bottom of a drawer to find it, because it's there in my little case – and I love it! It makes me so happy. I strutted around with that battery case on for days, feeling like a battery drug dealer. What do you want? AAs? AAAs?

We really treasure dinnertime as a family. Growing up, most of my best conversations with my parents happened around the dinner table – those are some of my favourite memories.

I want the boys to have fond memories of the family eating together, too. So, it's important for us all to sit down together at the end of the day.

Sometimes, it really is the first opportunity for us to talk to each other properly, because when the kids are back from school it's such a mad rush: they'll be running about outside, they do their homework, and they go off and play their games. Sitting down at the table means we all come together and catch up with each other properly: What have you done today? What's happening? And what's going on with you?!

Usually, I like the boys to eat dinner around six o'clock and Joe and I will eat with them, unless one of us is working and then we'll have something separately when we come home. Having an early dinner gives me time to then start getting Rex ready for bed, and for everything else that needs to happen in the evening.

♡ Who's In The Kitchen? ♡

Joe is a good cook and we'll share the cooking a lot of the time. Joe's got his staple recipes and he's a real carby cook. He doesn't think he's had a meal unless a full bowl of pasta or rice is involved! Nadia Sawalha taught him how to make what she calls 'mama spaghetti' – the easiest thing in the world, but so bloomin' tasty. You put a generous amount of tomato paste (I'd say about half a tube), a chopped-up onion, two cloves of crushed garlic and some olive oil in a pan, and stick that on the heat. Boil some pasta, then just chuck the pasta and some of the water into the tomato sauce that you've cooked – the starch in the pasta water thickens the sauce to make a lovely tomato pasta dish. The kids are obsessed with it and Joe loves making it. He loves making carbonara, too – none of the rest of us really enjoy carbonara, but we eat it for him because he does. You think, oh, he'll be upset if we don't love this as much he does!

As for me, I've never had any issues in terms of the boys' eating, but I think it's because I've never given them choice. I've never cooked meals on demand – I just cook what we've got. I think that comes from growing up that way. We never really had the luxury of even saying, 'Oh, I'd love *that* tonight, Mum.' Instead, dinner was whatever the hell my mum had – she just made it and we ate it.

How I Cook (A Confession)

I am really flexible with recipes – I might just see something once somewhere and think, that's a good idea. And then I'll just chuck in whatever the heck I want! I think most of the time with cooking, if you're not tasting it and adding what you think it needs, it will probably turn out rubbish. So, if a recipe sounds good, I'll take a quick glance at the ingredients and then I'll just make it the way that I like it. I think that's my best bit of advice with cooking: to just keep tasting your food and add whatever you want. Don't be too strict with recipes – or it might not turn out how *you* like it. So, if someone else uses 10g of butter but you prefer 25g, even if it's a little bit indulgent, I say, put 25g in – add what you think the food needs and keep going with it!

So long as the things that need to be cooked through are cooked through properly (no one wants food poisoning), you can't go too wrong.

♡ Hack Your Meal Healthy ♡

I thoroughly enjoy my vegetables. Still, even I know veg can be bland and boring. Sometimes I'll put a bit of chicken seasoning on my vegetables just to make them a bit more exciting, or I'll give the kids a blob of their favourite sauce or hummus on the side. For example, salmon and kale is one of their favourite dinners. But my eldest, Zach, won't eat the salmon unless he has a bit of mayonnaise to dip it in, because he thinks it's really boring without it. And I think, if he's eating a whole piece of salmon with just a tiny blob of mayonnaise each time, then I would much prefer that than him eating no salmon at all.

Tip If I boil some peas and carrots for a bit too long, they go a bit soggy and flavourless, and I know that my kids will go, urgh, Mum! That's when I say, 'Let's put on some magic salt.' It's just chicken seasoning – in my opinion, any kind of seasoning like that is just a load of salt – but we'll sprinkle some of that on, and they prefer it that way. Obviously, it's not good to have it all the time and loads of it, but I would rather the boys have a tiny sprinkle of salt on their veg than not eat it. And if they *still* wouldn't eat their veg? I would probably just soup everything – because my kids love a soup – with loads of flavour and stock and stuff like that.

Meal Time

OUR FRIDAY NIGHT FAVOURITE

The boys' favourite dinner is Jewish chicken soup, which we'd
have on a Friday. It's a clear chicken soup which you eat with
really skinny noodles, *lokshen*, and *kneidlach*, which are like
fluffy little dumplings. It's so yummy. You get a boiler chicken
(so it's got all the giblets in it, for flavour), put it in a big pan of
water and leave it simmering all day on a really low heat with an
onion, a couple of pieces of celery and a couple of carrots, all
chopped up, and some stock – I like Osem chicken flavour. The
chicken starts to fall off the bone – it's so good! – but you can
help it on its way with a fork if you need to. If you want to go all
out, you can make the *kneidlach* dumplings from scratch – but
you might find it easier to buy a mix and just add some eggs.
Then, about 20 minutes before you're going to serve the soup,
add your *kneidlach* so they boil in the pan. Meanwhile, boil up a
separate pan of *lokshen*. Once the noodles are ready, drain them,
put some in each bowl and add some soup and dumplings. (All
that's left in your big soup pan at the end is the carcass with the
giblets – you don't have to eat them, don't worry!)

For the soup itself, that's the traditional recipe given to me by my Nan – my dad's mum. He was born Jewish; and my mum converted to marry him. So, I definitely think of myself as Jewish and we observe the traditional holidays (more on those in the next chapter). I'm not kosher – which means I don't follow all of the rules – and I still love Christmas! But it means a lot to me.

Normally, my family would all take it in turns to host a traditional Friday night dinner and everyone would pile into each other's houses – my favourite thing in the world. When we're able to do that, I would usually give the boys the soup as soon as they come home from school instead of a snack, then a few hours later they'll have a full roast dinner – that's the Friday night dinner etiquette! But if we can't have a proper Friday night dinner, I would still give them the soup as a main with a couple of slices of bread. It's my favourite dinner, too.

NIGHT-BEFORE PREP

Aside from a proper sit-down meal, there are a few things I like to do in the evening, as part of my routine to help things run smoothly. But I do try really hard to get the boys to bed at a decent time and make sure they've got their stuff together before they do so, so that we can actually enjoy each other in the morning.

Every evening, if it's school the next day, my kids will pack their school bags and start to get their lunch ready. I'll tell them to choose their crisps, maybe a chocolate bar, a piece of fruit, put it in their lunchbox, and I'll shove in a sandwich in the morning. If they want chopped-up fruit, they can cut up their own, put it in a little container in the fridge and in the morning they can just add that to their bags, too. What that means is, I don't have to be rushing and chasing them the next day.

It doesn't always happen – some evenings I am working late, or I just can't be bothered to argue with them at nine o'clock at night when they're still not in bed and they haven't packed their bags. And the next morning, it's absolute carnage! But I do try to make it happen the night before. If you think about it, we only get that window in the morning and then a few hours when they get back from school to be together. I don't want to be arguing with them and have them thinking Mum is always moody.

As for me, sometimes I prep stuff the night before. Maybe if I'm going to work, I'll get my outfit and pack a bag ready for the morning. Or if we're going out for the day, say to the beach, I will get a beach bag ready. But that's about it. I find that sometimes if I prepare too much the night before, I end up forgetting stuff. On occasions, I've packed the baby bag thinking, we're going out tomorrow, and then the next day I forget to even bring it with me in the car! Because I've got ahead of myself – in my head I've already checked off that job. Whereas if I pack it in the morning, then I know I've got to take it. It's better for me to just wake up knowing that I've got to do a, b and c, because then I'll definitely do it all. It's just about finding out what works for you and what makes you happy.

♡ Wind-Down Time ♡

After dinner, we'll put on something that all the family can watch so the boys will chill out with us – and I'll get Pickle into his pyjamas and have him with us, too. When he wasn't sleeping through the night, I would put him down on his own, in his cot. But now that he's sleeping through, I can give him a cuddle on the sofa and he'll fall asleep.

I've never had a baby like Rex when it comes to sleep. He just takes himself into a corner when he's tired and goes to bed. It's hilarious. He'll often find a really tiny spot he can squeeze into, take his blanket, bunny and dummy and off he goes. Most recently, he's fallen in love with the dog bed, so we bought him his own one and it's his favourite place to have a nap.

Little things I love

When I get Rex into his pyjamas, I will also choose his clothes for the next day and put them on a little stand I bought for his bedroom. I get real joy from choosing an outfit and hanging it on there – it's one of my favourite things to do in the evening.

Little things I love: **Daims**

Ooh, I just love Daim bars – hard caramel inside and chocolate on the outside. I ate them when I was younger, then they went off the radar and I could never find them anywhere. Until my love for IKEA led me back to them! After leaving home and starting to shop there for my own place, I realised IKEA stocked them. Eventually, they started becoming available *everywhere*. And I'm so glad!

Snack Time

EASY BEDTIME TREATS

On occasions, I'll make the boys something sweet before bed –
and me and Joe, too.

Choc-banana milkshake: Blend some bananas with a few
scoops of vanilla ice cream – just add bananas or ice cream until
it's a consistency you like. Chuck a little whipped cream on the
top, with marshmallows and grated chocolate to finish.

Hot chocolate: Warm up some milk in a pan and stir in some
hot chocolate as the packet says – but to make it special, top with
whipped cream, marshmallows and grated chocolate.

Grown-up treats: Joe doesn't really like chocolate bars, so he
will have a glass of Coke and a biscuit – Oreos are his favourites.
And then I'll have a cup of tea and a Daim bar, of course.
We'll have those and watch a film – perfect.

Tidy
QUICK CLEAR UP

I cannot have toys out in the evening! While the older boys are getting ready for bed, any toys that still haven't been cleared up have to go away. Joe and I barely get a moment to sit down and watch something we want – normally it's *Peppa Pig*, or the boys' favourite computer game, Minecraft, will be on there. So for us, it's about shoving all of the toys into a basket and putting on telly we actually enjoy , so we feel like we have an adult home for an hour or two.

And, finally, it's just us – Joe and I get a bit of time for ourselves. It's one of those things that we actually ended up having a discussion about, because we weren't getting that time alone – at all. And it's a work in progress, even to this day. The boys were staying up later as they're getting older, we'd both have work, and it would get to half-nine, ten, and we'd just go to bed without time to ourselves – eventually we thought, this isn't healthy. We decided we need at least half an hour to an hour where we just sit down next to each other. So now, Leighton has until eight, sometimes it's half-eight, downstairs; Zach has until nine, until they go up. Zach's older now, so he still might stay up a bit in his room and play a computer game online with his friends or watch a film. That means even if Joe and I don't talk to each other and we just watch a film, we're still having some time for just us before bed.

Little things I love: **Being cooked for**

If I get home from work really late, Joe will wait for me before he eats – he'll feed the kids, then we'll have like a treat together on the sofa: a takeaway, or something that I really like. He knows what I love so he might warm up some chicken soup from the freezer, or make cheese and beans on toast. I know it's not really a dinner, but I love it!

Make Up

✂

PILLOWCASE DINNER TRAYS

I always wanted one of those cushioned dinner trays, and I wondered if I could make one myself... so I did. I was really proud of myself!

Old pillowcase
Stuffing
Picture or printout to fit the frame
Tray-sized frame (I wouldn't use a glass one, as it might get knocked about)
Glue gun (or hammer and small nails)
Drawer handles (optional)
A staple gun

1. First, cut your old pillowcase into two across the middle so that you have one half with three closed sides (and one half with two open sides).

2. Stuff the half with the three closed sides (don't stuff it too much, like I did! If you fill it too much, your tray won't sit comfortably on your lap).

3. You can fold the raw edge under to keep it looking neat.

4. Next, insert your picture of choice into the frame, and glue on your handles, if you want them. (If you're going to use your tray a lot, you might want to get a few small nails and hammer the pillow onto the frame, so it's a bit more hardwearing.)

5. Staple the stuffed cushion half to the back of the frame.

♥ ♥

♥ *Tip* You don't need to buy special cushion stuffing for craft projects. If you've got old clothes that you don't wear anymore, and they're not good enough to go to someone else or to charity – use them for stuffing. No one's gonna see them!

Frame

Eat me!

Stuffed pillowcase

Done ✔

♡ My Weekly Bathtime ♡ Ritual

I can sit in the bath for ages. If I get into it about eight, by the time I finish it, it's probably ten o'clock and I'll go straight for bed. So I only do it about once a week, as usually Joe and I are trying to have our time together in the evening – but when I do have a bath, I go all out. I call it my 'thrush bath' – because I put everything in it, and think oh my G-d, I'm probably going to get thrush!

The first thing I do is run the water – and when I have a bath, I run it scalding hot – there's nothing worse than a lukewarm bath. So, I make it really hot and then the process begins.

Step 1

Bath bomb. I am obsessed with bath bombs. I don't know whether it's because of the smell, the fizz, the colour, the glitter – they just give me life. So I search high and low for new and exciting bath bombs. I'll share some with you at the end of this.

Step 2

Soap/bath milk. Sprinkle in your favourite bubble bath – I love Wild and Wood powders, they are really sensitive on the skin.

Step 3

If you invest in anything for your bathroom, invest in a bath board. It's my favourite bathroom item. On it, I put flowers, candles, a Daim bar, and there's even a slot for my champagne flute of Diet Coke.

Step 4

Now, if you want to be extra posh, add rose petals. I want to pretend I'm in one of those posh hotels in Bali that everyone shows on Instagram. So I sprinkle dried petals and flowers all over the water, making sure they're the same colour as the bath bomb I've used. Be careful, though, because sometimes things on Instagram are not what they seem. Have you ever seen those pink thistle-type flowers that are all over Instagram when your favourite influencer goes to a posh retreat? Well, I tracked them down and bought them… and let me tell you, it was like bathing in broken glass. They scratched *everywhere*. I ended up with what I call Bali Thistle Rash – it was a nightmare. And worse still, I bought about ten bags of them because they came from so far away. So let me save you some money – and skin. Stick with rose petals.

Bath. *Done* ✔

Little things I love **Bath bombs**

I've tried lots of different brands, but the ones that make the best colours and make the bath look the nicest are from Lush – I like Big Blue. Or, there's a small business called Bridie's Bombs that makes the loveliest colours and smells, so I use those, too.

♥ ♥
♥*Tip* Afterwards, I have a better night's sleep – and it turns out a hot bath (or shower) really *can* help you sleep. I learned this from a sleep expert, Dr Sophie Bostock, I met through working with Benson Beds. She was brilliant. Apparently, it's because your body tries to cool you down from the heat of the bath, and the temperature drop makes you feel tired, helping prepare you for sleep.

♥ *Tidy* ♥
BATHTIME CLEAR UP

I reuse my petals, so while I'm still in the water, I will take them out and spread them around the side of the bath to let them dry. In the morning, I will put them back in their little petal tub, and then I'll tidy!

I don't use a lot of cleaning products, if I'm honest: I just use a multipurpose spray where the bath bomb's been, a sponge when I'm running the taps to wash it all away, and that's about it. I give the sink a good wipe down, too – I don't know what it is, if it's a boy thing or what – but when the boys brush their teeth, they spray everywhere, so I'll give the sink a rinse. And then I get out my bath bombs – but this time these are special ones you can get for the toilet! They're eco-friendly and fizzle up to make the toilet all nice and clean, so I'll finish with one of those.

Make Up

BATHROOM TIDY

I had a random piece of wood in the junk trunk – it had probably come off the side of something – and I thought, that could make a nice shelf! I just had to add a few bits...

Drill and drill bit
Small, flat piece of wood
Chunky piece of rope
8 little brass hooks
Stick-on hook

1. I drilled a hole either end of the wood, got some thick rope and threaded it through, tied a knot at each end, and that was it – I had a shelf ready to hang!

2. I also screwed eight little brass hooks into the bottom side, for my scented bath bags that I like, before I hung the shelf up on the wall by the rope. (I didn't want to drill into my bathroom tiles, but a really strong stick-on hook has been fine.) I arranged some bathroom bits and bobs on there and it's perfect.

Make Up

✂

JELLY SOAPS

This was a really fun one for the kids. Since we'd been washing our hands more than usual during lockdown, I said to the boys, 'Come on, let's make some soaps that you like. And if you made them, then you can use them every day!' It'd stop them from going through my liquid soap so fast, I hoped...

Half a cup of water
1 teaspoon of salt
2 sachets of gelatine powder
Half a cup of liquid soap
Dash of food colouring
Food moulds (or an ice-cube tray)

1. Boil the water in a pan before adding the salt, then take it off the heat and mix in the gelatine powder – that's what will make it wobble like a jelly.

2. Add the liquid soap and the food colouring (we used green).

3. Give it a good mix, then pour the liquid into your moulds: I used silicone ones that I already had for cooking.

4. Put them in the fridge to set (ours took about 20 minutes), then turn them out when they're no longer liquid.

♡ Bedtime Calm ♡

I keep my bedroom quite clear. Walking through the door I just need to see a bed and nothing else, ideally. So the most I ever have to do in my bedroom is hoover, wipe down the windowsills, maintain the few bits on the bedside table, and make my pillow spray if it's running out.

Tidy
DECLUTTER YOUR BRAIN!

That last tidy I do before bed is to tidy my brain. When I get under the covers, I can lie there for ages, thinking, I mustn't forget to do this tomorrow. And have I done that? Or, have I done enough for the boys or have I got that ready for school? And I'm just *worrying*. Sometimes I've had so much on my mind that I can't sleep.

I've heard lots of people say you should write down your thoughts and worries before you go to bed, to get them out of your head. So I started drawing a little dustbin – for my brain junk, I call it. I have to see things visualised in some way, or they don't make any sense to me. I've always been like that – for me, everything needs to be a picture. So now I just write all my

174

thoughts in that bin before bed. And then it's almost as if you're saying to yourself, 'Right, you've got all the junk onto the paper. Everything you're worried about, anything you might forget, it's all there. You don't need to think about it. The day is over, and you can just sleep easy...'

Feel free to take a pic and go to it on your phone every time you need to write something down.

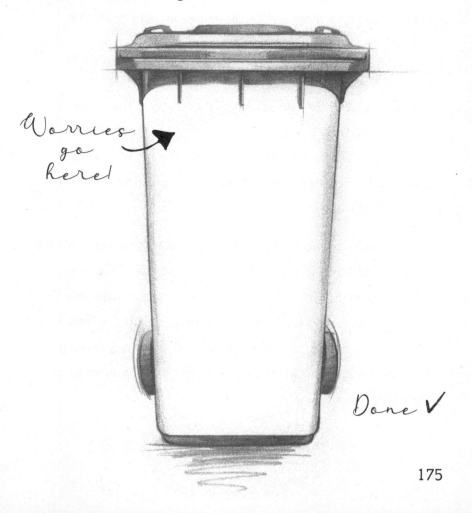

Make Up

DIY Dream Catcher

I love making my dream catchers – they're supposed to catch bad dreams, to help you snooze. I've made loads of them.

Yarn or string

A hoop (I just find them online by typing in 'dream catcher hoop').

Decorations: crystals/feathers/fake flowers

1. First, you wrap the yarn/string tightly around the hoop, to cover it. Start by tying one end of your yarn/string to the hoop to secure it, then cut and finish with another knot when the whole hoop is covered (trim the sticky-out bit of yarn/string that's left).

2. Next, you're going to weave the dream-catching net itself: tie the end of the roll of yarn/string onto the hoop. Once you know the technique, it's easy – you're going to pass this yarn/string around and back under the hoop, creating a little loop. And you'll do this several times around the hoop, leaving a few centimetres between each little knot, until you've gone all the way around.

3. Then, you just keep repeating this movement: but this time looping the yarn/string around the middle of each bit of the web you've already created. Carry on working your way to the centre and when the gaps in the net are getting really small, tie the yarn/string off and trim the end. Glue on your decorations however you like. I tied extra pieces of yarn/string to the bottom of the hoop so it hangs down like a fringe. Then hang the hoop on your bedroom wall with a bit more yarn/string tied to the hoop as a loop.

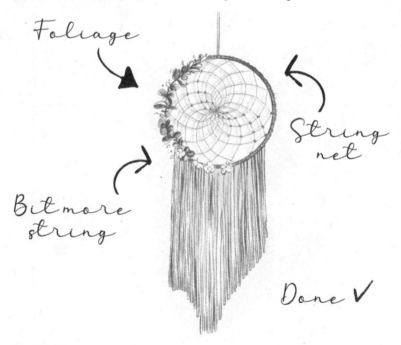

Foliage

String net

Bit more string

Done ✓

And now you've reached the end of the day with me. Give yourself a pat on the back – and good night!

Making Every Day Special

So far, I've shared my usual daily routine with you – but we're not finished yet. Of course, there are weekends, birthdays and holidays to think about, too – and for me, they're really special, because each one represents a chance to make memories I love.

And there's a lot of tidying, organising and crafting behind all that, too...

♡ Time For Family ♡

My weekend starts like the rest of the week – early! Sometimes Joe will take his little boy away for the weekend – he's older now, so Joe'll get in a little lie-in then. But Rex does not know what a lie-in is! And my body now wakes me up early anyway. So even if Pickle was to somehow sleep till ten, I'd still be up at six. But that's OK, because there's a lot I've got to fit in.

Every other weekend, our routine is that the older boys go to their dads' after school on a Friday and come back Sunday night. But if they're with me, then Saturday is our day, when we pick a place and go out and do something: a little trip. Then, if I haven't managed to get much time in for myself during the week, crafting-wise, I would dedicate some time to that on a Saturday. So, even if I take the boys out, I would come home and have a Saturday 'crafternoon', as I like to call it. Honestly, it makes Saturday feel like a proper day off!

Joe and I don't go out much at the weekend, to be honest. I know that sounds boring, but I don't love going out! If Joe and I really wanted to, then we would ask my mum to help with Rexy and try to get out. But the thing is, we've got four children between us and quite frankly, we're exhausted. So the very thought of getting dressed up, going out, having a drink, going to bed late, then waking up early with the kids is just not appealing. So we save nights out for special occasions and try to get a weekend of childcare in place so we can enjoy it. Saying that, though, we really like our kids and we like being around them. The three older boys are at an age where we have a laugh and we enjoy their company, so we don't crave a night out alone.

We love to get away as a family when we can. And, while I was writing this book, Joe's dream of owning a caravan came true! So now our family car is a campervan (yes, that's what we go to the shops in). It's a big old monster. You can fold down the back seat to make a bed and raise the roof to make space for another one up top, and we can all sleep in there. The kids love it – and, with a few essentials, I must admit I do, too.

MY MUST-HAVES FOR ROAD TRIPS

A car bin, which I find really useful. We got ours from eBay. It's basically just a little black bin that hangs on the back of a front seat and we can put all our rubbish in it. The built-in car bins are like an ash tray – far too small!

Car hooks – these attach to the bars of your head rest. So you can hang coats, bags, whatever on them, to keep everything off the floor.

iPad holder – this also clips onto the bars of your head rest, and it means the kids can watch a film on long journeys.

A mirror for Rex – he hates facing backwards in his car seat and not seeing anyone, so we bought a special mirror for his car seat and now he's happy!

Tidy
THE CAR

In the past, Joe and I have shared a car, and it never stayed tidy for long. He'd go away for work and leave his overnight things in the boot afterwards, or sometimes I'd find swimming bags that had been there for months. His way of dealing with things sometimes is to shut the door (or the car boot). I get that mentality – I can be like that, too! – but I'd often go in there and sort it all out. A lot of what we keep in the car doesn't need to be in there. Anything that does, I'd organise by category and put in separate bags in the boot. When we had our car, Joe would usually take it to get it cleaned, but if I decided it needed doing, I'd take out our cordless Hoover and give it all a good vacuum. Polish the surfaces with normal polish. Wipe inside and outside the windows with a bit of window cleaner. That's it! Our van's a lot harder to keep tidy than a car – it's a much bigger space, with a sink and a hob.

You've got to really think about what you cook in there, and then you've got to wash up everything straight away, otherwise it stinks! So wish us luck...

PREPPING FOR THE WEEK AHEAD

As well as our family time, I'll be organising, too. It makes everything go a bit more smoothly when we're back into the working week and the boys' school routine. But more importantly, as you know by now, I enjoy it!

So, normally, the routine is that we do our big food shop on a Saturday – or we'll occasionally do an online shop that will arrive that day. Then Sunday is my day to get ready for the week ahead – which includes meal prepping. It's life-changing. I'm not even joking!

Basically, I cut up a load of vegetables that I'll use in the week for soup, and dip into that throughout the week for the kids, too: if Pickle wants a snack during the day, I'll just grab him something from that vegetable pot in the fridge. I also cut up a salad – it doesn't necessarily last the whole week, because we all eat it, but I probably get a good three to four days out of it (and that also means we're not trying to finish off slimy lettuce on a Friday, when it's a bit tired). I'll also try to prep a few dinners for us: say, for Monday, Tuesday and Wednesday.

So, to prep one meal, I might put chicken in one pot and marinate it on a Sunday, peel potatoes, cut up my veg so it's ready to cook, and put it all in the fridge in containers labelled 'Monday'. That means I know that when I make dinner on Monday night, all I've got to do is just add the veg and potatoes to a pan and chuck the chicken in the oven; and I'll do the same for Tuesday and Wednesday, too. When I get home from work or if I've had a long day with the baby, sometimes I really don't want to start peeling potatoes, and knowing that I have a meal almost ready is just the best feeling ever.

I feel like I'm still making fresh food, but I'm not having to do it every single day. It does mean that most weeks I know exactly what we're going to be having to eat, if I'm cooking – but I can switch it up a bit. I can always have Tuesday on a Monday!

My top tips for keeping your prepped fruit and veg fresh

♥ Chopped veggies like carrots, potatoes and celery are best kept in water. Change out the water every couple of days to keep them going even longer.

♥ The best way to keep your salad crisp is to transfer it into a clean bowl, cover it with kitchen roll and then add a layer of cling film – make it as secure as possible to stop the air getting in and the leaves wilting.

♡ Leftover freshly chopped herbs can be saved in your freezer. Pop them in an ice-cube tray, top it up with water and have handy herb cubes ready to defrost when you need them next.

♡ Lemon and lime wedges are at their best when they're juicy. To keep them that way, you'll need to cover them as quickly as possible. Wrap them tightly and individually in cling film or a reusable stretch food cover to store them in the fridge for a few days. To keep them for longer, you can use a cupcake tray as a substitute ice-cube tray – place each wedge separately in a hole, cover it with water and store in the freezer.

♡ To improve the lifespan of your fruit and veg more generally, make sure you don't store them together! Quite a few different fruits (apples, avocados and bananas, for instance) produce ethylene gas, and this can cause other fruit and veg around them to ripen faster.

♡ When I can, I always like to swap out cling film with reusable stretch covers/lids to make it more eco-friendly.

♡ Ready For Refill Hour ♡

Sunday is also one of my favourite days because I refill *everything* – all my jars, containers and dispensers – and make sure we're all stocked up for the week ahead. So I refill all my candles in my wax melts, all my cleaning and detergent bottles from the big bulk packets I use, all of my diffusers, even the egg holder and the bread bin – just anything I can think of in the house!

I genuinely enjoy the whole process of refill. And it doesn't have to be Sunday, of course – you could do whatever suits your routine, and you might find a Monday evening, say, is the perfect time for you to do it. But it works really well to have a bit of time to get everything refilled, and then you don't have to think about running out of anything all week.

Tidy
THE FRIDGE

The fridge always gets tidied on Sunday, too. I try to use everything I've got in my fridge through the week before, so I can tidy and refill it along with refill hour. I will pull everything out, give the fridge itself a good clean, check the dates on everything I've got out, and put everything back that's still good to eat. The things that aren't in date I try to use up in what I call a 'mouldy veg dinner', featuring everything that's in the fridge that needs eating (it's not really mouldy – I wouldn't recommend that – but it's veg and bits that are still OK to eat, but aren't the freshest).

I chuck them into a pan and make something out of them, whether it's mouldy veg soup, a mouldy veg Bolognese, a mouldy veg stew – anything, just to make sure I use everything up.

Tip Get a glass bottle you can fill from the tap and keep that in the fridge. In my house, everyone loves to drink from the chilled bottle – it makes it more special than getting it straight from the tap.

187

♡ Bigging Up The Birthday Plans ♡

With so many kids and me and Joe, there are a lot of birthdays to celebrate in our family. I do like to make a big thing of birthdays for the boys and I would always have some sort of theme, based on what they're into at the time. They've had Ninja Turtles, Star Wars, Lego. And I'll carry that theme – or its colours – through their presents, cake, snacks, party bags (if you're making them). It just makes it that bit more special, but you don't need to spend a lot, and it doesn't need to be perfect.

For example, for Rex's birthday, I did a green and white jungle theme because he had some jungle teddies already. To start with, I hung a monkey teddy from his high chair, and put a stuffed lion next to his cake. I tied a load of green, white and gold balloons together for an arch, and I used white, green and brown paper for his presents. And I decorated the egg-shaped chair that he likes to sit in with fake leaves and flowers, to make it fit the theme.

I made a cake, too, but it was terrible – it had two tiers and looked like the Leaning Tower of Pisa! I covered it up with a few fake leaves.

That is one thing I'm not very good at, celebration cakes. I can make a cheesecake, I can make a sponge, but when it comes to decorating them, I'm not brilliant. It doesn't really matter! (For Leighton's birthday during lockdown, I couldn't get hold of a Pokémon cake for him – so I ended up decorating my own with radishes. The boys just found it really funny.) But best of all was Rex's donut wall…

Make Up

DONUT WALL

Donut walls can cost a fortune to buy; making one probably cost me a fiver. (As for the pegs, you can take the glue sticks off the board at the end and shove them back in a glue gun when you need them – the spray paint does wash off, if you're worried about it showing when you use the glue sticks.)

Cardboard box (you want to save a slim, squarish or rectangular one that you can stand up, ideally. You can always cut one down to size if not, though)
Glue sticks for a glue gun
Spray paint
Label
Fake foliage
Donuts!

1. Starting with a cardboard box I'd saved, I stuck on glue sticks on one side as pegs – they're what you buy to fill a glue gun, but they're not sticky until they're heated up (so I used my glue gun to stick each one).

2. I chopped mine into smaller pieces so they weren't sticking

out too far, but you could use pretty much anything you liked as pegs as long as they are the right shape.

3. Then, I spray painted the whole thing black, stuck a label on it (mine are always from my sister; I'd ordered one saying 'Donut grow up'), added some fake foliage, for Rex's green jungle theme, and hung my donuts straight on it on the actual day. I thought that was a really nice, easy idea.

Foliage

Box

Donut Grow Up

Glue sticks

Done ✔

Spray paint

191

HUNGRY CATERPILLAR

All the boys have had a hungry caterpillar for their first birthday – and it's so easy.

Seedless green grapes, cut in half (please google how to cut a
grape in half safely for children)
A tomato
Miniature sweetcorn
A few blueberries

1. Arrange the halved green grapes on a plate in a slightly wiggly line, for the caterpillar's body.

2. Cut a round slice off the side of a tomato, keeping the skin on, and place it face down at one end – that's the head!

3. Add slivers of purple grapes for the feet and horns. Finish with slices of miniature sweetcorn with a blueberry on each one for the eyes, and a little blueberry piece for the nose. You can make a sun out of miniature sweetcorn slices, too – arrange them in a circle in one corner of the plate and scatter a few around it for its rays.

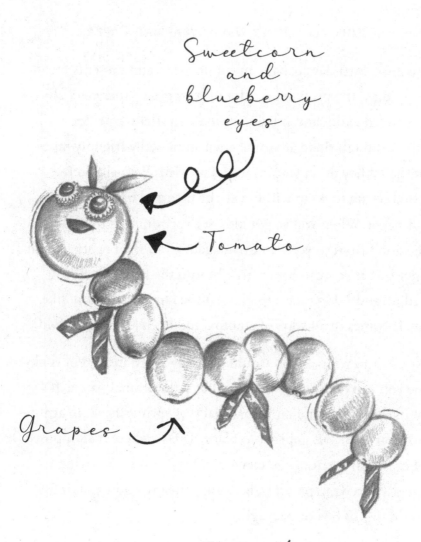

Sweetcorn
and
blueberry
eyes

Tomato

Grapes

Done ✔

WHY YOU DON'T NEED WRAPPING PAPER

Of course, birthdays usually mean presents, and presents mean wrapping… the problem is, a lot of wrapping paper can't always be recycled easily, and it being covered in sticky tape doesn't help. Although there are some environmentally-friendly tapes out there, they don't stick as well. I've tried them all! So I've started trying to wrap without sticky tape and using recycled craft paper. When you've got kids, it's very difficult to make sure they don't rip it so you can use it again – but the beauty of craft paper is that you can put it straight into the recycling, if you need to, and I don't have to pick off the tape or anything like that. It comes in all sorts of colours, and it's really easy to fold.

Just use it to wrap as you would normally, then instead of sticky tape you can tie it up with string, like a traditional parcel. It's not like a slippery, metallic material that springs back up again – once you fold craft paper into place, it stays where it's supposed to be. The string, too, you can reuse: I try to save the string I have used to wrap presents, because I already know that it fits a certain size of box or packaging.

♥ ♥

❧ *Tip* I use fully biodegradable balloons these days. They don't have that oily, plasticky finish of the balloons you usually see – but the kids don't care!

194

Make Up

BIRTHDAY CARD BOOK

Birthday cards
Hole punch
String

On Rex's first birthday, I really wanted to keep all his cards afterwards, so this is what I came up with. Stack your cards inside one another, starting from big on the outside to the smallest in the middle, then hole punch through all of them. Tie them together with a bit of string, and you've made a little birthday card book. I keep it in Rex's memory box so when he's older – or whenever I want to, more like! – we can look through them together.

P.S. I made a photobook of his first birthday, too, using one of the companies that advertise online. They were one of the cheapest ones I found and the result was really good quality, even though all the pictures were just taken on my phone – I don't have a professional camera. So, don't think those are just for weddings: you can use them to remember special birthdays and other events, too.

♡

Seasonal
Tap to Tidys

If birthdays are a big deal for me, it's gonna come as no surprise that I like to go all out on other occasions, too! Honestly, I just love to make memories all year round. So now, I'm gonna share with you some of the crafty ways I do that...

♡ Christmas Starts ♡ Early...

Christmas is a really big event in our house – and I start months ahead! I use reusable advent calendars – wooden frames with pegs to hang a little bag for each day of advent. I start filling them with mini versions of the boys' favourite chocolates or sweets, and little personal things, too. If I ever go to a big department store, I'll try to blag some mini aftershaves, so I can collect as many as I can throughout the year, and I'll put them into their advent bags as well. And then I will go online sometimes, too, to look for miniature versions of things they love: key rings that look like mini PlayStations, or anything else mini that I can find.

I'll start getting presents early on in the year, too. When I first had Zach, it was just not feasible to get to December and suddenly buy a load of presents for Christmas. I had to sort of work my way through the year, buying little bits and pieces here and there, otherwise I just couldn't afford it. Even now I feel like it's just a bit too much if I don't, in terms of the pressure to get loads of stuff. Also, I do feel like prices go up closer to Christmas: you think, hold on, that was two pounds six months ago, and now it's more than double! So I buy little bits and pieces throughout the year.

... BUT I TRY NOT TO GO MAD!

I spoil my nieces probably more than my own kids, if I'm completely honest with you!

I'm quite funny with my children and presents, because I think if they have too much to open on the day, they just end up opening stuff, putting it to one side, opening more stuff and not even appreciating what they've just got. I have to really rein Joe in as well, because he could just go mad if I let him! And, because I'm separated from the older boys' dads, they then have another whole day where they get spoiled absolutely rotten – and rightly so! But it does make me think about what I give them, otherwise it would just be a free-for-all.

So, I only really get little stocking fillers for the boys for Christmas Day – a pack of chocolate pennies, some new socks or a little mini Lego set to build, and that kind of thing – and one main present, too. A few years ago, Leighton's main present would have been a new bike or a new scooter. And then Zach loved Lego for a long time: every year he'd get a big set that was really bloomin' expensive. Now they're getting older, they tend to want vouchers. It saves me a hell of a load of wrapping, and it also makes them a bit more responsible because they've got to make decisions on how to spend a voucher – they learn that once it's gone, it's gone. Whereas sometimes I think if it's all bought for them, they might not appreciate it as much.

PUT YOUR OWN TWIST ON TRADITION

I love Christmas food, but feel free to tweak it. None of my kids eat mince pies, and I don't like them – so I make apple and cinnamon ones. None of my kids eat Christmas pudding, either – but I love the way that it lights up when you pour the brandy over it and set it on fire! So we make a version that's not made out of fruit cake but is more of a treacle-y pudding. And our Brussels sprouts are always cooked with loads of butter, bacon and chestnuts.

Meal Time

STACEY SPROUTS

Few rashers of bacon, chopped
Brussels sprouts
Spoonful of butter
Handful of roasted chestnuts

1. First, fry off some chopped-up bacon, then add a bit of water to the pan to make a bit of salty bacon juice (it'll be nicer than it sounds, I promise!).

2. Meanwhile, in a separate pan of water, boil the Brussels – not until they're mush, but for about seven minutes so they're still crunchy but not raw.

3. Drain them (saving a bit of the water), cut them in half once they've cooled a bit, then add them to the pan with the bacon.

4. Lace all that with a tiny bit of the saved Brussels water and a big heaped spoonful of butter, and simmer for probably six to eight minutes.

5. Roasting chestnuts takes a bit too long for me, so I just buy them already cooked, then add them to the sprouts in an ovenproof dish. And that's it! Just chuck it all in the oven for about 10 minutes (keep watching them) so the sprouts crisp up.

CHRISTMAS CANDY CANE HEART LOLLIES

Of course, Christmas isn't just about the dinner – there are so many chances to make fun snacks and treats, too.

Lolly sticks
Two miniature candy canes (per lolly)
Two boiled sweets (per lolly)

Space your lolly sticks out on a sheet of greased parchment paper set on a baking sheet. Arrange two mini candy canes either side of each one, to make a heart shape at the top of the stick. Within each half of the heart, place a boiled sweet. Put them in the oven at 180 degrees C for 2 minutes, until the sweets have melted. Remove from the oven and leave to cool on the baking sheet.

Done ✔

Boiled
sweets

Candy
canes

Snack Time

MINI CHRISTMAS PUDDING CRISPY TREATS

Half a pack of mini marshmallows
Coco Pops (or use Rice Krispies and a few chunks of chocolate)
Pack of hard white icing
Handful of redcurrants (or another red berry)
Small mint leaves

1. Warm up your marshmallows in a heatproof bowl set over a pan of simmering water, stirring occasionally.

2. When they've melted, stir in your Coco Pops. As you know, I don't measure anything, so I would add enough cereal so that the mix is sticky, but not watery, or too dry. (You can also make this with Rice Krispies – just stir in some chunks of chocolate after you've added the Krispies, so they melt and turn the mix brown.)

3. Next, take the bowl off the heat and let it cool down a little.

4. Then, really wet your hands and grab a small, golf ball-sized amount – roll it around in your hands in a circle, to make a neater ball. (If you don't wet your hands, the mixture just sticks to everything.)

5. When you've made all your balls, let them set a little bit – on a wire rack or a sheet of greased parchment paper – then with clean hands, mould your hard icing into little puddle shapes.

6. Put one piece of icing on top of each ball and finish it off with a redcurrant – although any kind of edible, small red berry will do – and a small piece of mint for a tiny 'holly' leaf.

P.S. You can adapt this recipe to make mini cornflake wreaths. Just swap the Coco Pops for cornflakes and add some drops of green food colouring to the mix. Let it cool, then instead of making balls, flatten them into more of a donut shape – poking a hole in the middle of each one. Add three little redcurrants at the bottom of each (if you do it while it's wet, they will just stick), for holly berries.

♥ ♥

♥ *Tip* Even though parchment paper is supposed to be non-stick, I always find that if you grease it as well, you've got a better chance of things coming off it easily.

Snack Time

MINI HOT CHOCOLATE MARSHMALLOWS

Chocolate buttons
White marshmallows (big and mini)
Miniature candy canes

Put a chocolate button on top of a big marshmallow – that's going to be the cup filled with hot chocolate – and hang a tiny candy cane off the side, for the handle. Top each one with cut-up mini marshmallows. You could stick it all together with icing, but you can also just make them 'loose', so the kids can pick them apart. It just depends what they like – Zachy doesn't like his stuck down, so he can eat a bit at a time!

Chocolate button

Marshmallows

Candy cane

Done ✔

Snack Time

CHRISTMAS TREE PASTRY

Puff pastry
Jar of pesto
Grated cheese
Egg wash (mix an egg with about a tablespoon of milk or water)

1. Cut a sheet of puff pastry into a large, slim triangle for a tree shape, put onto a baking tray, then cover it in pesto.

2. Sprinkle with loads of cheese, then cover all that with another piece of pastry – cut into the same triangular tree shape.

3. Next, cut diagonal lines down each side of the tree, but don't let the 'arms' meet in the middle.

4. Working around the pastry, take two arms and twist them together, then do the next two: these are going to be its branches.

5. Use a pastry brush, if you've got one, to cover the top of the pastry with egg wash (to give it that nice glossy look), then bake for 25 minutes at 200 degrees C or until the pastry is golden brown and looks cooked through (a little bit flaky). If you lift the pastry up with a spatula, you can see if the pastry is cooked underneath.

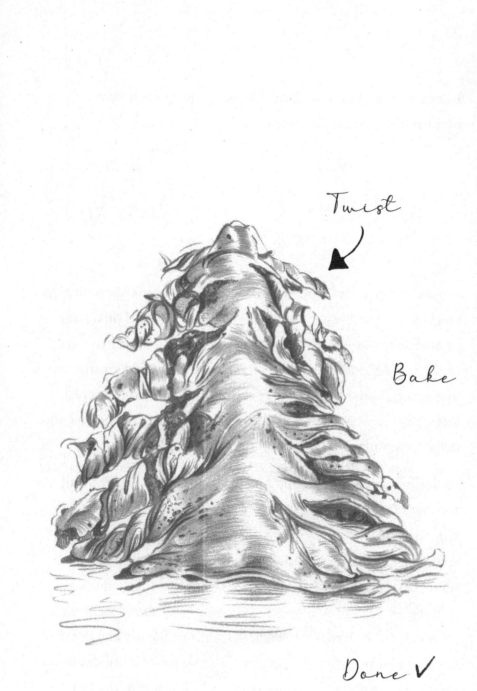

Twist

Bake

Done ✔

But maybe the best bits of my Christmas prep are how much opportunity there is for crafting.

♡ Why I Never Buy Crackers ♡

I make my own crackers, because I genuinely think shop-bought crackers are terrible – even when you spend 25 quid on a pack of posh crackers (which I think is an absolute joke) all you get in there is a bloomin' pencil or a miniature bowling set that no one's ever going to use. It's a load of rubbish! So, I order cracker kits online in September, when they tend to be a bit cheaper and definitely available.

Basically, you get the snappy stick, joke and a hat (paper, so all recyclable), as well as a paper wrapper for the cracker itself. All you need to do is add your own gift: so if I know my mum's favourite chocolate is a Daim bar, I can put a mini Daim bar in there. I can even do what I do with advent calendars and put mini tester perfumes in there – everyone loves those! Personally, I'd much rather have a mini Chanel scent inside my cracker than another bloomin' thimble. Or, let's say you go on a holiday and they've got really nice shampoo and conditioners in the hotel –

save up the freebies and use them as cracker prizes at Christmas. It doesn't even have to be a present: you could write a little message to each person if you wanted. And even if you spent money on miniatures, it should still work out a lot better value per cracker – better bang for your buck, if you like. And yes, they do still bang if you make them from a kit!

Make Up

CHRISTMAS WREATHS

I love making my own wreaths. I always use stuff I can pull apart and use again after Christmas.

A decorative hoop
Fake foliage and flowers
Any decorations/spray snow

1. Just start with a hoop – you can find them online for a couple of quid. Then, I'd wrap it with a garland of plain (fake) fir.

2. You could add some fake flowers in there, too. Most fake flowers and garlands come with some sort of wire stem, so I tend to wrap it around my wreath and that's all you need to do. You can even go out to the woods and get some real fir cones and acorns, and add a bit of spray snow if you like. (I'd use a really small amount of glue so I could take them off after, because I do like to change up my wreath.)

P.S. You can make a stair garland similar to the wreath. I bought a long fir garland which I wrap around my staircase and that looks really nice. Because it's wire-based, it does just stay the way you've placed it. Then add some string lights – for a couple of quid, you can get really thin LED ones that won't show the wire.

Hoop

Foliage

Spray snow

Done ✔

Make Up

WOOLLY CHRISTMAS TREE GARLAND

A small piece of card (about 10cm by 6cm. I've used Joe's
passport in the past!)
Green wool
Wool in a complementary colour and decorative beads (optional)

1. For this garland, you're going to make lots of little woollen Christmas trees. Holding your card upright, get your ball of green wool and start wrapping it around the card (around the longest part) about 20 times.

2. Once you've done that, trim the wool off from the ball.

3. Then, cut along the pieces of wool at one edge of the card (carefully holding the wool in place, so it doesn't go everywhere). Now, you've got loads of pieces of wool folded in half.

4. Use one piece to tie around the top uncut end, about 3cm down. It looks a bit like an octopus with loads of little legs, but that's one tier of your tree!

5. Do that two more times, to make three tiers. (Ideally, you want your tiers to range from big to small: if you don't want to fiddle with different-sized cards, trim two of them just a little.)

6. Then, ruffling out its 'legs' to access the middle of the smallest tier, glue the medium-sized one up into it. Then do the same with the big one: glue it into the underside of the medium-sized one. You've got a tree!

7. If you gently pull one of the pieces of wool at the top of the tree a bit loose, it makes a loop so that you can thread each tree you make onto a longer piece of wool. Once you've got a few on there, it makes a really cute Christmas tree garland.

8. You can use the same green wool throughout, but I might use green to make the trees, then thread them onto white wool, adding white beads between each tree. To hang the garland up, I'd just place its ends under ornaments on the mantelpiece.

Make Up

PERSONALISED CHRISTMAS BAUBLES

Empty baubles
Filling of your choice
Label maker (optional)
Ribbon

So a really fun thing to do at Christmas is to make your own baubles. You can buy clear empty baubles online quite cheaply if you have a hunt. Then you can just fill them with the things that you love. I filled one with little crystals – they're only cheap – one with glitter and one with fake flowers (of course I got in some fejkas!). I finished mine off with little labels, just from one of those label makers that print them out as you type, with messages like 'Merry Christmas Susan!' (remember her?!) and 'Pickles 2020'. You can say whatever you want! And I found a bit of black ribbon – but you could use whatever matched your Christmas colour scheme that year – and tied that to each bauble, then you're done. So easy!

Make Up

NORM THE GNOME BAUBLES

I'll get to big Norm in a moment... but I actually think these are the cutest things ever.

Felt or cardboard to make a cone
String
Scrap of fake fur
Tiny pompom

Use your felt or cardboard to make a small cone shape. Put a little loop of string inside the top of the cone you've just rolled up (just glue or tape it in) so you can hang it from the tree, then glue the edges of the cone together. Next, cut a bit of fur into a triangle and stick that on the front, for the beard. Glue on a tiny pompom for the nose. And that's it! They're so easy, but I love them.

Tip Recently I wanted to go black and white for my Christmas colour scheme, but I didn't want to buy a whole load of new baubles. So I decided to just spray paint a lot of the baubles I had in my new theme colours. Why not?! You could also put a load of glue around them, dip 'em in glitter, or wrap them in ribbon that you like – anything you fancy!

Make Up

MINI STANDALONE CHRISTMAS TREES

A4 piece of green card
Decorations of your choice
Small stick and small, round piece of wood (optional)

1. Roll your piece of card into a cone shape (for this, I just roll the rectangular A4 piece without cutting it first. The bottom won't be flat – one edge will hang down more – so trim that with scissors so the cone is more even. It doesn't have to be perfect!).

2. Then, decorate your green cone, by gluing on whatever you like! You could wrap some pretty yarn or ribbon around it, stick on pompoms, sprinkle it with glitter, add an old piece of jewellery – like a diamond earring (fake, of course!) – at the top for a 'star'. You've got a little Christmas tree!

3. It will stand alone, or you can glue a small stick (I use a diffuser stick – trim it down if it looks too tall) upright onto a little round piece of wood.

4. Place your tree on that, so the stick goes up the middle of the cone, and it looks like the tree's on a little stand.

P.S. You can also do a pine cone version of this: instead of a paper cone, glue a pine cone onto your wood slice. I decorated one with little stick-on pearls, which I loved. And if you buy some scented pine cones to make a few of these, they will smell amazing – it's almost like having potpourri around, but in a really nice, stylish way.

♥ ♥

♥ *Tip* You can buy the little round pieces of wood I use here (they're called craft wood slices, or rounds, if you look online). But, if you ever have a small fallen tree or stump in your garden, you can literally just saw that into slices. (I would always paint them with what you treat garden decking with – an oil or stain – for a nicer finish.) Once they're dry, you can use them for all sorts of crafts. You can make placemats out of them, coasters, anything – so never throw away a fallen tree!

Yarn

Pompoms

Stick   Cone

Done ✓

Craft wood slice

217

Make Up

FESTIVE WOODLAND TREE FRAME

Small sticks or pieces of wood, in a range of different sizes
A4 canvas
Miniature fairy lights (battery-powered)

Arrange the small sticks or pieces of wood on the canvas horizontally, from small at the top to big on the bottom, to make a tree shape (leave a bit of space between each one). Place another small stick or piece of wood underneath, positioned vertically. That's your Christmas tree branches and trunk! Once you like how you've arranged them, add the fairy lights. The battery pack's going to go behind the canvas, so make a small hole (use a screwdriver) at the end of where each 'branch' starts and ends. Then, thread the end of the fairy lights through the canvas, and wrap the wire around each stick or piece of wood, taking it back through the canvas after each one (so you don't have lights showing between the branches). Glue down each branch onto the canvas as you go. Once you've done them all, just switch the lights on!

Fairy lights

Canvas

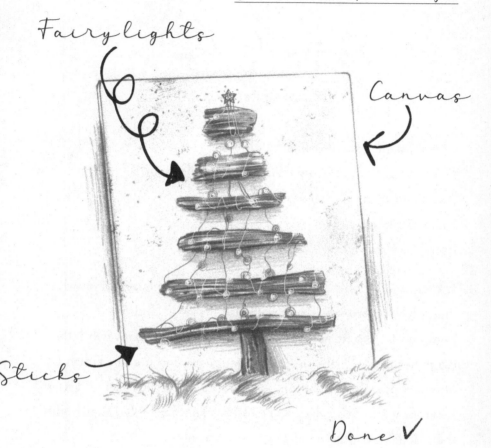

Sticks

Done ✔

Tip Everyone loves leaving out a mince pie for Santa and carrots for his reindeer, so why not make up a plate for him, too? I like to order little labels to section off a special plate for Santa, with spaces marked for 'carrots', 'pie', 'glass of milk'. My older boys still really get into it, even if it's just for me. They'll go outside, put the plate out, look out the window, and say, 'I think I saw him, Mum!'

Make Up

REINDEER PRESENT JARS

Clean Nutella jars and lids (or similar)
Three mini pompoms (two white, one red) per jar
Two small twigs per jar
Piece of ribbon per jar
Paper label/tag per jar

Take an old Nutella jar that's clean and with its label removed, then glue on two white pompoms for the eyes, and a red pompom for the nose. For the reindeer horns, glue on two little twigs to the top of the jar, so they stick up into the air. Finish by gluing a piece of ribbon around the rim of the lid, and add a label for whoever's going to receive it. The boys filled theirs with their dads' favourite chocolates for Christmas.

♥ ♥

♥ Tip I find gingerbread houses really difficult to make. So, one thing that's fun to do with kids is to try making a healthy gingerbread house. Cut, say, carrots and celery into batons, then use the carrots to build four little walls and the celery to create a roof – with hummus to stick it all together. You could even decorate it with tomato windows or cucumber doors. If that sounds a bit daunting, just do it flat on a plate!

Little things I love:

Christmas Eve boxes

... or really, I should say this is something the boys absolutely love – so I love doing them, too. They have a Christmas Eve box every year. It's a wooden box I can reuse, and it will contain their new Christmas pyjamas, probably a pair of slippers and maybe some chocolate coins or hot chocolate mix or another treat to make up that night.

♡ *Feeling Festive* ♡
All Year Round

Of course, Christmas isn't the only opportunity to get organised and crafty throughout the year. As I mentioned, we celebrate our Jewish holidays, too. One of the big holidays in our year will be Purim, because the kids love it. They get to dress up as their favourite character – the idea is that they have to hide themselves in disguise. It's a long story! That falls around Book Week in school, so they get dressed up twice, which I love. And Rosh Hashanah – Jewish New Year – is important to us. It leads up to a big family Yom Kippur meal, and we'll have some honey and apple, which is traditional. Hanukkah we always mark, too: the boys love it because they're supposed to get a gift every night of the festival, though it will only be small. And we'll get the menorah out – the special candle holder we use – and I'll decorate a Hanukkah table in blue and white for the eight days of the festival, too.

You may have your own traditions and holidays, but whatever they are, it's lovely to make special things to celebrate them. Here are a few quick little ideas to get you started…

♥ ♥

♥ *Tip* A really nice way to mark the change of seasons is to have a seasonal display in one corner. Mine stands on a lovely slab of wood on our side table next to the sofa. (I won't tell you how we found the slab or it came into my possession, because I'm not sure we're entirely allowed to have it! But we do have it and we love it, and we're looking after it.) For autumn, I arrange my dried grasses in vases, and put a little pumpkin on there, adding some dried flowers in autumnal colours, too. For winter, I change it all up for some (fake) winter plants from Primark – holly, ferns, that kind of stuff – with a Christmas candle and a festive Norm. In spring, I like to do fresh flowers in little vases, and for summer, sunflowers always.

♡ Easter ♡

We do a lot of crafts for Easter, making bunnies and crispy chocolate nests. And for Rex's first Easter, I got him a bunny outfit with floppy ears – it made me so happy!

Make Up

EASTER CHICK JAR

This is a fun, easy one to do with kids.

Clean jar
Yellow spray paint
Felt tip pens or markers (black and orange, if you've got them)

Spray paint a clean jar yellow, then draw on black dots for eyes and a little orange triangle for a beak. Fill it with Easter treats!

Snack Time

EASTER CHOCOLATE POTS

Small, clean plant pots
Chocolate cake or similar (anything sweet, brown and crumbly
*   will do)*
A small carrot per pot

Another thing I love to do is to make edible plant pots: you can
buy a little plant pot or use your old ones (just make sure to wash
them out thoroughly). Fill them with edible 'soil', your crumbled-
up chocolate cake or whatever. Finish by burying a real carrot!

♡

Snack Time

EASTER BUNNY TOAST

Slice of toast
A little oil, for cooking
Egg
Cucumber and Coco Pops, to finish

Cut a rabbit-head shape from the centre of a piece of toast (I just used a knife. I have a thousand cookie cutters but not one bunny one, believe it or not! But a bunny head is easy – it's just an oval, with two long ears on the top). Put the toast with the hole in a pan coated with a little bit of oil and push down firmly. You're going to add the egg to cook it just like you would do a fried egg – but pour the white of your egg into the bunny shape first, before adding the yolk separately, so you can position it as the bunny's nose. Once cooked, carefully remove from the pan and finish with thin strips of cucumber for some cute whiskers, and a couple of Coco Pops for eyes (you could use raisins or anything like that, though).

Make Up

RABBIT SOCK BUNNY

*Old sock (I like spring colours like yellows and duck-egg blues,
    but you could do little black or white bunnies if they're the
    socks you've got lying around!)*
Uncooked dry rice
Couple of elastic hairbands
Ribbon, to decorate

Cut off the end of the sock under the heel, and fill it with rice.
Then tie a hairband around the middle to make the bunny's body,
and tie another hairband around the sock a bit higher up, to make
its head (keep a bit more rice in the bottom half, so the body's
bigger than the head). The leftover bit of material at the top is
going to be the bunny's ears – just cut the spare material in half
(up to where it goes into the hairband). Then shape each half into
a long ear shape (you could sew around the edges, or glue them
into place). Finish with a cute ribbon bow around its neck.

Tip I love an Easter wreath – especially if it looks like a bunny in bloom! Buy three twig wreaths, one larger than the others. The biggest is going to be the bunny's body, a smaller one its head. Cut the third wreath into two halves and bend them a bit straighter – they're going to be the bunny ears (just trim them if they're a bit too long). Glue it all together, then cover the whole thing in fake flowers, lightly gluing them on so you can pull them off and reuse them later.

Make Up

EASTER EGG FAVOURS

Plastic eggs (you can buy crafty ones that open into two halves)
Yarn or string
Fake flowers, to decorate

Cover the outside of each half of your egg with a bit of glue, then carefully coil yarn or string (I like the natural-looking twine) around it, until it's all covered. I will stick a few flowers on there, too, and the eggs look really pretty arranged in a basket. You can put treats inside them, and use them as favours for the Easter table.

♡ Autumn And Halloween ♡

I prefer pretty autumn decorations to Halloween ones, but my kids love the scary stuff. So, I have autumn decorations out right until the very end of October, then we get spooky...

Make Up

UNICORN PUMPKIN

Kids' unicorn headband
Pumpkin
Fake flowers, to decorate
Pair of fake eyelashes

This definitely falls in the pretty category! I made this with my nieces: we got hold of a headband with a unicorn horn and ears – anything from a pound shop or online is fine. You need to cut the ears and horn off the headband, stick them on the pumpkin, glue on a few fake flowers running from the top and down the side as a mane, and finish with a pair of eyelashes. And you're done! You don't have to be really artistic, just have fun with it. My nieces were just over the moon with this.

Tip If you buy pumpkins early, say mid-September to the end of September, they shouldn't go off before October – pumpkins can last for months if they're not carved up. If you're just leaving them whole to decorate your front steps outside, or using them as table decorations (or dressing one up like a unicorn!), they should be totally fine. And if your pumpkins are lasting well past Halloween, you can always turn them into Christmas reindeer! Just follow the unicorn make up (see left), but using some antlers from a novelty headband instead. Or, call your local homeless shelter and check if they'd like some pumpkins – a lot of the time they will take them.

Horn

Eyelashes

Pumpkin

Done ✓

229

Snack Time

SWEET POTATO PUMPKINS

Sweet potato(es)

Slice each sweet potato into chunky slices. Use a knife to cut out smiley faces from some (so they look like mini Halloween pumpkins) and use a small leaf-shape cutter on the others (keeping the outlines, as well as the inside leaf shape bit). Cook on a baking sheet in the oven at 200 degrees C for 20 minutes. That's it!

Snack Time

RICE KRISPIE PUMPKINS

Marshmallows and Rice Krispies

Orange food colouring

Chocolate Matchmaker sticks (or similar), cut into shorter 'stalks'

1. For an autumn twist on crispy treats, melt your marshmallow and Rice Krispie mix as you did for the Mini Christmas Pudding Crispy Treats recipe on page 203 (but without melting in the chocolate).

2. Add a few drops of orange food colouring, then shape chunks into slightly flattened balls: pumpkins. Top each one with a short piece of Matchmaker 'stalk'.

Make Up

SEASONAL LANTERNS

Clean glass jars
Autumn leaves
Mod Podge (this stuff works like glue, but seals things a bit
  like a varnish, too)
String
Electric tea lights

These were so easy and fun to make. First, I washed the labels
off some old pickle jars with warm water and soap, and spread
out my (real) leaves to make sure they were dry. I stuck the leaves
onto the jars with Mod Podge, then covered them in more Mod
Podge so they wouldn't rot. I tied some string around the jar tops
to decorate, then added candles/tea lights inside. (I wouldn't use
real candles for these because the glass and leaves could get too
hot – just use fake electric tea lights!)

Leaves

Mod
Podge

Done ✔

Make Up

SOCK PUMPKIN

Old sock (orange, if possible)
Stuffing (I've used uncooked dry rice)
Needle and thread
Spray paint/fake leaf, to decorate

Cut your sock off under the heel, then fill the foot that's left with a few centimetres of your stuffing. Tie the end in a knot and cut off the leftover bit of sock material. You've now got a little ball – give it a squeeze so it's a bit more pumpkin-shaped. Then, start sewing your thread around it: put your needle through the bottom and up through the middle of your pumpkin, then pull it back around the side before going up through the bottom again. Keep doing this to make eight little pumpkin 'segments', going back through the middle each time, and pulling the thread tight. To finish, I spray painted an old fejka leaf gold and glued it on the top!

Sock

Thread

Done ✓

Make Up

No-Sew Gnome

An old sock or an old pair of tights
Uncooked dry rice
Scraps of fabric for his legs and hat
Some sort of stuffing
A scrap of white fake fur
A miniature pompom

I wanted to make a cute Halloween gnome and I do love him
– he's my little mate, Norm! Cut the foot off an old sock or one
tights leg, fill it with dry rice and tie it at the top – that's his
body. If you like, you can cut scraps of fabric and fold them
together to make two little matching legs sticking out underneath
(just glue them into place to keep them from unrolling). Then, cut
a triangle from a scrap of fabric – I used an old orange jumper
of Rex's that didn't fit him anymore – and make that into a cone,
gluing the edges together to make the cone shape.

Next, stuff the cone. I used a bit of fake fur that I already had,
but you could use anything you've got lying around. Then you
just stick the cone (the hat) onto the body. Glue on a triangle of
white fake fur for the beard and add a little pompom for his nose
– I didn't have any in, so I stuffed a scrap of an old beige sock,

to make a nose. Halloween Norm's got autumnal colours, with a black and white stripy body, and an orange hat, but you could change the colours to red and green to make a Christmas Norm. It's up to you!

Tip Cones are difficult for a lot of people to get right in crafting. And even Norm's hat doesn't look that great, if I'm honest! There are lots of different ways of making cones, depending on what material you're using. If you're not sure what's best, there are loads of videos online that show you different methods to try. Or, if you can't get the cone right, buy a little cardboard one from somewhere like Hobbycraft to wrap your material around.

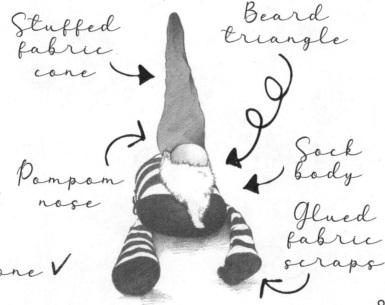

Stuffed fabric cone

Beard triangle

Pompom nose

Sock body

Glued fabric scraps

Done ✓

Bat Treats

Oreo cookies
Reese's peanut butter cups minis
Icing googly 'eyes' (find them in a supermarket)

Snap an Oreo cookie in half and press the halves into the top of a peanut butter cup, to look like little wings. Finish each with a pair of googly 'eyes'!

Oreo halves

Reese's

Done ✔

SNACK CUPBOARD TIDY

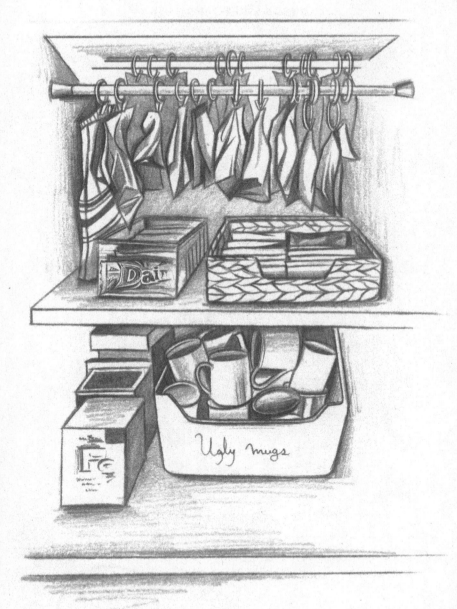

Done ✓

238

Tap to Tidy Q&A

Before I go, I want to answer a few of the questions that I always get in my messages...

Q. The number one question I always get asked is, where do all your leftovers go when you're refilling all your food jars?

A. As I've now revealed (!), I keep all the food I've bought in bulk in the plinth drawers in the kitchen. But you can put them anywhere you like, if you want to do the same: a dry shed, the utility, a cupboard. All you need to be able to see is the food you've got in your containers – you can hide the rest!

Q. Are you always tidy?

A. As you might have realised by now... absolutely not. The likely reality in the kitchen, say, is that a few cupboards will be tidy, because I've recently spent time on them. And the rest may be absolute mayhem! It can't all be perfect all the time.

Q. And does it stay tidy once you've organised something?

A. No – but I thoroughly enjoy keeping it up most of the time (not always!). After a few weeks, everyone's been in and out of a cupboard, someone's put something back in the wrong place, *I've* put stuff back in a lazy order. But I do enjoy having time to myself and putting it back to rights. Also, once you've got systems set up, putting it back is much easier, because you've already got a place for everything. So when you put it all back, you never think, I don't know what to do with this – and there's probably a container with a label on it to help you, too! You can just chuck it straight in there, in the place you've already picked for it. The maintenance is much easier after the first tidy, I promise.

Q. Why do you always have to do something? Why can't you just do *nothing*?

A. I get a lot of messages like this! The truth is, I do sometimes think, oh, I can't wait to just sit on the sofa and do nothing. But actually, what I've found out about myself is, I don't really enjoy doing nothing. And it's not like I want to fill my spare half an hour with my tax return! I want to do something that I enjoy, even if it's colouring-in, or organising something for me. It's all about finding out what makes *you* happy, and not worrying what other people think about what you're doing.

Q. How do you deal with trolls?

A. So as some of you may already know, there are lots of people out there who really don't like me. The truth is, that's OK. I can't change those people – and why would I? Everyone is entitled to their opinion, even if it's really nasty. It says way more about them than me. I like to think of it in this way: nobody has the power to make me feel a certain way unless I give it to them. And I refuse to give it to them. I must protect my happiness at all costs, and never compromise it. If you remember one thing from this book, remember how incredible you are, how strong you are, and how nobody – and I mean NOBODY – has the right to make you feel any less. Don't let them take back the power!

A Final Thought ♡

Before I end this book, there are a few things that I just have to say.

Everything written in this book is an ideal. It is what can be achieved when everything is running perfectly. The truth is, it is impossible to believe that anyone could live their life like this, day in, day out, with no questions asked. Life is unpredictable. Children are all-consuming and, especially right now, the world is unlike anything we've experienced before. Well, in my lifetime anyway. Structure and routine are harder than ever to put in place. So if you get anything from this book, I hope it's this: you are more than enough. You don't need to be tidy, organised, the queen of crafts to be winning at life. You just need to be you.

Although I've shared with you the things that help me stay sane and give me purpose, there really is no manual for life. And you just have to do what is right for you and your world. Don't worry about those who think you're too clean, not clean enough, obsessive and over-organised, or scatty. Too big, too small, too happy all the time. Or miserable. You can never please all of the people all of the time – and why would you want to? Take a look at your unit, and at yourself, and ask, 'are we happy?' If the answer is yes, then sod the rest of them.

It really has been an intense year and, quite frankly, you've done incredibly. So, if some of these Tap to Tidys bring you comfort and joy, then woohoo. But equally, if you need to shut the door on life and say, 'not today', woohoo to that, too.

Every day you get up, show up and give everything you can, regardless of how exhausted, sad, angry or hopeless you feel. That is enough. Just to get up, show up and be there, day in, day out – that is the biggest achievement, if you ask me.

Even if nothing else gets done that day, that's OK. You've already smashed it.

If you've read this book, I hope at some point in the near future you get a moment to yourself to enjoy the craft, or a 'thrush bath', or even to organise your stationery. And I hope that it brings you as much joy as it does me, because despite what you tell yourself, you deserve it – and much more.

My final, final thought: there will always be people in life who treat you like you're not good enough. They'll make you feel like you weren't born in the right postcode, or you didn't make the right choices in life, like you don't belong in their world because of who you are (and these are the people who pretend to stand for everyone), those who pretend they're the women supporting women type of people... Let me tell you something from the bottom of my heart. Because you need to know. Coming from someone who's felt this way throughout my whole life/career... F**k them. You're perfect. Where you came from, grew up, the level of education you got, the choices you made good or bad, your accent, how you look, just everything about you is what makes you YOU and that is so special. Go out and GET IT yourself. You don't need their help. You can achieve it without them, I promise you. And you'll help everyone you can in the process. And when you get to where you deserve to be, those pretend people soon want to know you then. Which will give you the PERFECT opportunity to smile and walk away from their double standards, and live your life YOUR way with your head as high as the sky and moral compass intact.

Love you to the moon and back,

Stace xxx

♡ Acknowledgements ♡

Thank you to Laura, Steph, Abby, Alice, Claire, Lou, Hannah, Aslan and the team at Ebury for believing in my book and actually publishing it. Woohoo!

Thank you to Molly, Blaise, Russell and Amanda at YMU Group for putting up with my ridiculously drawn-out edits, rewrites and constant perfectionism. A special thanks to Amanda for finding a publisher that believes in me and giving up your days to get it right.

Thank you to Emma Rowley for giving me the structure and helping me put down on the page exactly what's in my head, even when it didn't make sense to anyone but me.

Thank you to the incredibly talented illustrators who I wouldn't have met without Instagram. You have no idea how you've made my visions come to life.

The Famo: Mum, Dad, Karen, Jemma, Matthew, Joshy, SamSam, Ray, Aaron, Kiffy, Sharna, Casie and Dan, I love you all to the moon and back. I wouldn't be who I am today without you.

Joe AKA Hoe: only joking Bubs. You know I'm rubbish about being serious with you, but if you can't be mushy in an acknowledgement, when can you be? You are my lobster. I'm so grateful to have you, you are the most incredible male role model in our boys' lives. You do so much for all of us without wanting anything in return. Your love for us gives us the strength to follow our dreams and believe in ourselves. And I'm so happy I found you. Love you to the moon and back, Bubs.

Zachary, Leighton and Rex: boys, there are no words. All I have to say is this: it is all for you. It always has been, and it forever will be. To the moon and back, boys.

INSPIRATION LIST

Nothing can be made without inspiration, so thank you to all of the people, places, forums and websites that have inspired me.

Laleh – @jacobs_food_diaries
@5.min.crafts
Louise – @louloulikes
Kayleigh – @athomeohkaye
Saira – @sairas_life

Teresa – @mrsclarkescleaning
Mrs D – @mrs.ds.cleaning.reviews
Lauren – @madhouse063
Donna – @mrs_houseproud_
Sophie – @mrshinchhome

And, of course, Pinterest and Google – what would I do without you?

♡ Small Businesses ♡ Shoutout

I just love you, small business owners. Keep doing what you're doing. There are so many I want to talk about but I can't get you all in the book! So here are my favourite top twenties at the time of writing this – please check them out and enjoy!

HOME FRAGRANCE

D.S. & DURGA – @dsanddurga

Earth by Jennifer Sarah – @earthbyjs

Arran Sense of Scotland – @arransenseofscotland

Little Esscents – @littleesscents

BABLE Candles – @bableit

Waxaroma – @waxaromaldn

Homes with Nomes – @homeswithnomes

Grass & Co. – @grass_andco

Koko Rose Wax Co – @kokorosewaxco

Daisy Lane – @daisylanewax

Clueless Candles – @cluelesscandles

Made By Yasmin – @madebyyasmin

Sienna Heather Aromas – @siennaheatheraromas

Craze Candles – @crazecandles

Ell's Smells Wax Melts – @ellssmellswaxmelts
MYSA Box – @mysaboxuk
Candles by GLOW – @candlesbyglow._
Young Mary's – @itsyoungmarys
Village Wax Melts – @villagewaxmelts
Daily Flame – @dailyflame__

HOME ACCESSORIES

Maison White – @maisonwhite
Once Upon a Mural – @onceuponamural
By Bon Homie – @by.bonhomie
Mud Goods – @mudgoods
Crafty Mummy of 3 – @craftymummyof3
Red Candy – @redcandyuk
The Cheshire Gift Company – @thecheshiregiftcompany
Little Love of Mine – @littleloveofmine_
Ash + Olive Co – @ashandoliveco
Shower Gem – @showergem
Woody Marvellous – @woodymarvellous
Tolly McRae – @tollymcrae
Tea and Biscuit design – @teaandbiscuit.design
Ink Prints – @_inkprints
Milly Sands – @millysandsinteriors
Nuwe Roam – @nuweroam

And the Little Things – @andthelittlethingshome
Benji's Shop – @benjis_shop
Palm and Wild – @palmandwild
Everlee Olive – @everleeolivecreations
Where The Wild Girls Are – @wherethewild_girlsare
xNoahsArkt – @xnoahsarkt
SevenSeventeen – @sevenseventeenuk

CLOTHES AND SHOES

Beija London – @beijalondon
Sincerely Nude – @sincerelynude
Little Sweetie – @littlesweetie10
Dot & Bill – @dotandbill
The Tired Mama Collection – @thetiredmamacollection
Mamawears – @mamawearsgina
Laundry Day Clothing – @laundrydayclothinguk
Sargasso & Grey – @sargassoandgrey
Clothes Doctor – @clothes.doctor
VelveLuxe London – @velveluxe
Fennec and Darwin – @fennecanddarwin_fashion
Nicola Sexton – @nicolasextonofficial
Lolly Loves – @__lollyloves
Kitch Clothing – @kitch_clothing
She By Sophie – @shebysophie

Foxy Frox – @foxyfrox
WileyCubOfficial – @wileycubofficial
VerityAnne – @verityanneclothing
Neverfullydressed – @neverfullydressed
Wednesday's Girl – @wednesdays_girl

KIDS

Squelch Wellies – @squelchwellies
Pebble – @pebblechild
Kidly – @wearekidly
Fall with Grace – @fall_withgrace
Molly-Meg – @molly_meg_
SoFi – @sofishop.uk
Bellybambino – @bellybambinobasket
Ella Siena Children's Boutique – @ellasienaboutique
Mr Wolf Kids – @mr_wolf_kids
JuJuni – @jujunikids
La La Loop – @la_la_loop
Lana Nicole – @lananicoleclothing
Ivy Lace – @ivylace.uk
Noah and Moon – @noahandmoon
Craftly – @craftly
Education4All – @education4all
Crafty Pods – @craftypodsuk
Fanacapan – @fan.acapan

Two Little Acorns – @twolittleacornsofficial
Turtle & Badger – @turtleandbadger

BABY

Hallie & Harlow – @halliwandharlow
Daisies & Dinosaurs – @daisies_and_dinosaurs_decor
Crane and Kind – @craneandkind
Tiddlers and Nippers – @tiddlers_and_nippers
Baby Box – @baby_box.co.uk
Tilda Loves Teddy – @tilda_loves_teddy
My Baby Label – @mybabylabelx
Immy and Reubs – @immyandreubs
Wexbaby – @wexbaby
Another Fox – @another.fox
Amber and Noah – @amber.andnoah
The Little Realm – @the.little.realm
Baby Peanut Designs – @babypeanutdesigns
Rowan & Me – @rowan_and_me
Wear It Baby – @wearitbabyy
Alice Lily – @alice.lily.xx
Wild Slumber – @wild_slumber
Jelly Legs – @jellylegsuk
Mimmo Baby – @mimmobaby
Flicka – @flicka_norwich
Cuddledry – @cuddledry

FOOD AND NUTRITION

Pots for Tots – @pots_for_tots
Gardners Cookies – @gardnerscookies
Greedy Pig Food – @greedypigfood
Yasmin Alexander – @nutritionbyyasmin
Rebecca Wilson – @whatmummymakes
Chirky – @eatchirky
The Plattery & Vital Meals – @theplattery
Brittany Mullins – @eatingbirdfood
Beth Le Manach – @entertainingwithbeth
Little Cooks Co – @littlecooksco
Teeny Weany Takeaway – @teenyweanytakeaway
Scrumbles Cake Shop – @scrumblescakeshop
Scrumptious By Lucy – @scrumptiousbylucy
Cookie Caramba – @cookiecaramba
Cocoa Delicious – @cocoadelicious01
Just Got Snacked – @justgotsnacked
Rudy's Pizza – @wearerudyspizza
Rhiannon Lambert – @rhitrition
The Purple Spatula – @thepurplespatula_
The Whimsical Cakery – @thewhimsicalcakery

Jewellery and Accessories

Murray and Me Jewellery – @murrayandme_jewellery

Wilde Creations – @wildcreationsuk

India & Clay – @indiaandclay

Miss Clemmie – @miss_clemmie_accessories

The Bobby Pin – @thebobbypinuk

Zodiaq Ldn – @zodiaqldn

My Bags of Stuff – @mybagsofstuff

Omolola Jewellery – @omololajewellery

KaysDesigns – @kays_designs_

Seafoam Jewellery – @seafoam_jewellery

Blue Barkes Jewellery – @bluebarkesjewellery

Bee and Bloom – @beeandbloom_designs

Little Luxe – @thelittleluxeco

Makai – @makai_collective

Charlie Feist – @charliefeist

Geminite – @geminite_studio

Buzz Jolie Jewellery – @buzzjoliejewellery

Constellations London – @constellationslondon

Milly Grace – @millygracejewellery

Alex Monroe – @alexmonroejewellery

Hair and Skincare

Deviant Skincare – @deviantskincare

Pestle & Mortar – @pestleandmortarcosmetics

Graces London – @graceslondon

Liha – @lihabeauty

Wild Seed Botanicals – @wildseedbotanicals

Glow Beauty By Lily – @glowbeautybylily

Kaloneu – @kaloneu

The Big Silk – @thebigsilk

Soul Cap – @soulcapofficial

Alchemy Haircare – @alchemy_haircare

Plenaire – @plenaire_official

Narloa – @narloa

Celf Haircare – @celfhaircare_official

Candour Beauty – @candourbeautyofficial

Skin + Me – @skinandmehq

The Drug.Store – @thedrug.store

Mum Bub Hub CIC – @mumbubhub

Wild Science Lab – @wildsciencelab

Saint Iris – @saintirisadriatica

Mr Blackman's – @mrblackmans

BATH AND BEAUTY

Dani Levi – @itsdanilevi

BeautyLashUs – @beautylashus_

Dream Beauty – @dreambeautyltd_

Lauren's Luxuries – @laurens_luxuries1

Plush Brushes – @plushbrushes

Kitmate UK – @kitmateuk

Botanical Baths – @botanical_baths

Stylpro UK – @stylpro_uk

Booteek – @booteek_uk

My Kit Co – @mykitco

Bossy Glossy – @_bossyglossy

Telle Moi Nail Polish – @tellemoi

Wild + Wood UK – @wildandwooduk

CLS Nail Supplies – @clsnailsupplies

Oh Yours Beauty – @ohyoursbeauty

Bridie's Bombs – @bridies_bombs

Mellie's Bath Bombs – @melliesbathbombs

Icey Nailz – @icey_nailz_x

Lavella Beauty – @lavella_beauty

LuLu Letterbox – @lulugiftstore

CRAFTS

Craft and Crumb – @craft_crumb

MadeWithLove Crafts – @madewithlove_crafts_ie
&Designs

Wool Couture Company – @woolcouture

Crafts With Love – @craftswithlovexo

MessyMakersBox – @messymakersbox

Crazy Crafts – @crazycraftsltd

Childs Play – @childsplay_uk_

Crafty Macks – @craftymackswoodengifts

Clay Charms Craft Supplies – @crafty.mood

Crayation Station – @crayationstation

Glitter Glitter on the Wall – @glitterglitteronthewall

Katies Cottage Crafts – @katies.cottage.crafts

Eliza Henri Craft Supply – @elizahenri.co.uk

Party In-A-Box – @party_in_a_box_uk

Live, Laugh, Love with Lauren – @livelaughlovewithlauren

Lovely Little Lino – @lovelylittlelino

Little Brian Paint Sticks – @littlebrianpaintsticks

SnowWindows – @snowwindows

The Original Party Bag – @theoriginalpartybag
Company   company

Sculpd – @sculpdit

♡

If you scan this QR code, you can
access my Spotify playlist of tunes
to tidy and craft to – enjoy! Xx

Ebury Press an imprint of Ebury Publishing,
20 Vauxhall Bridge Road,
London SW1V 2SA

Ebury Press is part of the Penguin Random House group of companies
whose addresses can be found at global.penguinrandomhouse.com

Penguin
Random House
UK

First published by Ebury Press in 2021

www.penguin.co.uk

A CIP catalogue record for this book is available from the British Library

ISBN 978 1 52910 949 8

Typeset by seagulls.net
Printed in Italy by Elcograf S.p.A.

The authorised representative in the EEA is Penguin Random House Ireland,
Morrison Chambers, 32 Nassau Street, Dublin D02 YH68

MIX
Paper from
responsible sources
FSC
www.fsc.org FSC® C018179

Penguin Random House is committed to a sustainable future
for our business, our readers and our planet. This book is
made from Forest Stewardship Council® certified paper.